NONFICTION BOOK PROPOSALS

ANYBODY CAN WRITE

How to get a contract and an advance before writing your book

ELIZABETH LYON

Blue Heron Publishing, Inc. • Hillsboro, Oregon

Nonfiction Book Proposals Anybody Can Write: How to Get a Contract and Advance Before Writing Your Book. Copyright © 1995 by Elizabeth Lyon. All rights reserved. No part of this book may be reproduced, stored in a retrieval system, or transmitted in any form or by any means without permission in writing from the publisher, except by a reviewer, who may quote briefly in review.

Printed and bound in the United States of America.

Published by
Blue Heron Publishing, Inc.
24450 Northwest Hansen Road
Hillsboro, Oregon 97124
503.621.3911

First edition.

ISBN 0-936085-31-2

Publisher's Cataloging-in-Publication Data

Lyon, Elizabeth.
  Nonfiction Book Proposals Anybody Can Write / by
    Elizabeth Lyon. — 1st ed.
      p.   cm.
  Includes bibliographical references and index.
  ISBN 0-936085-31-2
  1. How-to. 2. Nonfiction book proposals.
3. Marketing I. Title

This book is dedicated to
the memory of R. Gaines Smith,
writing teacher, mentor, and best friend.

Acknowledgements

Writing any book is a monumental task and I have been especially blessed to have the help, encouragement, and love of many. My thanks to:

Dennis and Linny Stovall, the co-publishers of Blue Heron Publishing who believed in this book enough to make it a reality; literary agent and friend Natasha Kern who over many years shared her knowledge and experience about proposals and publishing; literary agent Denise Marcil who was the synapse that sparked my connection to the Stovalls; author and special friend Carolyn Cotter; the writers whose proposals are an integral part of this book; National Writers Club; and everyone who offered an endorsement.

Every writer needs a good editor. If editors were a measure of wealth, I'm the richest person in the world. My deepest thanks go to Patty Hyatt, Stew Meyers, and Carolyn Rose, all three "editor bears." Without their incisive editing and continual support, this book would have been a shadow of its current clarity and potential.

A special thanks to Aline Prince and Bill McConochie for reading and offering their critiques. For endless constructive criticism, I am grateful beyond words to Colonyhouse friends, to Victor Rozek, and to my critique group members past and present, including:

Monday group: Pat Swope, Patsy Hand, Therese Engelmann, Julie

Mathieu, Milt & Kathleen Cunningham, Fran Toobert, Jeanette Jacot, Trish Bradbury, Patty Hyatt, Chuck Ferree, Paul Brooks;

Wednesday groups: Aline Prince, Carolyn Cotter, Shirley Foster, Dennis Newman, Ellen Spear, Jan Johnson, Chris Bell, Geraldine Moreno-Black, Jane Van Dusen, Sarah Vail, Bill Lynch, Jerry Wolfe, John Dewitz, Carol Craig, Laine Stambaugh, Chuck Hitt, Elaine Stec, Caroline Wolfram, Charley Snellings, David Waggoner, Carolyn Rose, Mike Nettleton, Barbara Pope;

Thursday group: Bill McConochie, Michael Taylor, Evan Gentry, DeLora Jenkins, Barbara Stevens-Newcomb, Kassy Daggett, Dean Scoville, and Pat Phillips.

My family endured a particular strain during the pressured time period during which this book was produced. They give new meaning to unconditional love over the long haul of my writing career. Deepest thanks go to my parents, Don and Ella Redditt, to my children, Kris and Elaine Lyon, to my future husband, Charley Snellings, and to his daughter Sara. I give special thanks to my former husband, Louis Lyon, for years of believing in me and for his support.

Contents

Foreword

When Elizabeth Lyon first told me she was planning to write a book about how to write and submit nonfiction book proposals, I was delighted. I had long felt I needed specific guidelines for my clients and prospective clients and found existing books to be inadequate. I had contemplated writing a book myself, but knew that I would never be able to take the time from agenting and parenting to do the job. I knew Elizabeth was exactly the right person because I had sold several of the proposals she had worked on and mentored. They were far superior to the usual submissions we receive. My assistant had attended some of her workshops and found them to be invaluable. In addition, I knew that Elizabeth's teaching expertise would lead her to organize the needed information in an accessible and under-standable way.

There are many reasons why you would undertake the major work involved in writing a book. You may believe it will assist you with career advancement in another field; you may want to establish a new career as a writer; you may feel passionately and often altruistically that a certain subject must be presented to the public; and, you may believe publication will be a road to fame, fortune, self-understanding or a legacy of your life's work.

Most writers are usually not prepared for the challenge of researching and writing a proposal. You may think this is a task that agents will do for you. Some writers resist the necessity of treating this literary child of the heart and mind as part of a business plan. Often, some parts of the pro-posal process are troublesome. They can't get the right slant or positioning for their book; they have trouble organizing mountains of research mate-rial; or they find it difficult to write a positive bio touting their own accom-plishments. In some cases, they discover they are really experts and not writers at all. Perhaps they need to work with a coauthor or ghost writer. The services of an editor of Elizabeth's stature are invaluable in helping writers to achieve their goals and grapple with the problems they encounter in moving from expert to author.

One of the things that is most important in going through this daunting process is to continually refocus on why you are doing this and clarify your goals. Eventually, if you get an agent, you will need to communicate these goals to her so she can help you to get what you want from publishers. This focus will also keep your sense of commitment to and passion for your subject alive. It is important to keep in mind that the process of selling something to someone else is not a matter of convincing someone to buy something they *don't* need or want. It is rather a process of sharing your vision so clearly that the other person is swept up in it, experiences a contagion of your passion and excitement, and wants to share it with others. You want the agent or editor to wish your book were already written so they could share it with a friend or loved one or benefit from it themselves. When you begin to feel overwhelmed by the information you are accumulating about the market, publicity, chapter organization and so on, when your book begins to seem like a term paper, always come back to what prompted you to start this process in the first place and tell us about that.

I have never worked with a writer on a proposal without the writer feeling, at some point, that the effort was too hard or not worth it. There is always a point where it seems easier to give up. Yet, also without exception, writers have said at the end of the process of developing a proposal that they understood their books far better than they had before and were far more prepared to write them. Even authors of self-published books that have done well and are being presented to the industry gain new insights and often decide on revisions when they are thinking about how to tell editors why their books are new, better, different, more timely or more insightful than other books available.

This book is an invaluable tool for achieving success as a nonfiction writer. There is no substitute for paying attention to what those in this arcane industry tell you. I am invariably appalled when I receive query letters from writers who have had their work read and rejected by agents and editors for sound reasons and yet have ignored the advice they have been offered. Sometimes, they will send copies of rejection letters written by colleagues of mine who have taken the trouble to provide them with good advice about how to refine, refocus or further develop their projects. They believe that they simply haven't contacted the right person who is going to accept what they have written without requesting revisions. Pay attention to professionals in the industry rather than relatives and friends. In this book, Elizabeth has produced a compendium of methods and insights about getting published successfully that will spare you many problems on the road to publication. Read it through. Then proceed in exactly the order she has presented. Even if you determine that your project is not suitable for publication, you will have been spared much fruitless time and effort.

When you finish the steps she has outlined, you will at the very least have a preliminary proposal that will be understood and taken seriously. Chances are, you will join the ranks of the many writers she has helped to achieve publication. She is providing you with a set of keys to the fulfillment of your dream. Follow her advice so your dream can become a reality.

Natasha Kern, Literary Agent
Portland, Oregon, 4-30-95

A Note to My Readers

As an editor and instructor, I've watched students and clients struggle to decipher the basic steps of writing proposals. As a writer and author, I've had to do the same—picking my way along with little help from inadequate sources.

For years, how to write a nonfiction book proposal—or even the necessity of one—has been insider's knowledge. This book demystifies a process that has remained largely unexplained by the pundits of the publishing industry.

I've assumed that you know *nothing* about proposals and little, if anything, about the publishing world. As a result, I have organized this book in the order of reader need.

> Subjects include self-help, history, travel science, biography, naturopathy, psychology, personal experience, education, parenting, new age, writing, medicine, real estate, language, and more.

At each step in the process, I've interwoven examples from nearly two dozen proposals that span a variety of nonfiction subjects.

No need to flip to the back of a book to try to match instruction with examples. The proposals used in this book represent different stages in the marketing process; many exemplify published books, while others are currently being marketed by agents, and yet others are newly finished. The most important criteria is that a proposal serve as a good example. This book's appendix indicates each proposal's status at the time of publication.

I've designed the chapters to help you conserve your time and energy while enjoying the greatest productivity and quality. Each chapter begins with a statement of goals and a definition of terms. Each section of the proposal is covered in its own chapter. I've also included a troubleshooting section in most chapters. The final chapters of this book show you how to assemble, polish, and market your proposal.

I use a writing style that features headings, boxes, and bulleted lists in order to make the presented information easier to absorb. This style also allows you to come back later to easily find answers without having to cull through lengthy unbroken text. Sidebars provide accessible summaries and reviews for experienced proposal writers.

While this book supplies the recipe for a proposal, you are the one who must go into your writer's den, combine the ingredients, and create one. Like bread dough, proposals take kneading, putting aside to rise, and kneading again.

Over the years of helping writers as an editor and "book doctor," I've identified those qualities you must possess to write a successful proposal and book. You need a willingness to follow directions, accept criticism, and rewrite. Finally, you must persist until you succeed, believing in yourself and your idea.

CHAPTER ONE

Book Proposals: What Are They? Why Use Them?

Chapter Goal: To introduce and define proposals, explain who uses them, and present an overview of the publishing industry.

It's a great time to be a writer. It's an even better time to give birth to a nonfiction book. Never before have so many channels existed for publishing. Since the sixties, publishing has grown into a mega-industry with annual sales of over $16 billion. Practically speaking, about 20,000 publishers now supply the reading public. From large conglomerates like Random House to regional publishers like Blue Heron—the publisher of this book—a publisher exists to match virtually every reader's—and writer's—preferences.

Amazingly, the number of books published annually in North America has doubled in the last thirty years, to an average of 50,000 titles. In most years, about 85 percent of those titles are nonfiction. About 75 percent of those are by first-time authors. In other words, nearly 32,000 nonfiction books are written annually by first-time authors. Sidebar 1-1 reveals the size and potential of the publishing industry.

It's a great time to break in. A solid idea, the ability to communicate, and a well-written book proposal supply the practical means to that dream.

Not that you won't face competition. At a recent writer's conference, literary agent Mary Alice Kier of Cine/Lit Representation described a sales trip she made with her associate, Anna Cottle, to a dozen New York publishers. "With just about every editor we visited, there was a ritual held during the first five minutes before we could sit down: clearing boxes of manuscripts off chairs or moving them to give us room for our feet. In some instances, our meeting was not held in the office." Not, she explained, due to the widely held myth about power lunches to cut deals

Fascinating Facts About the Publishing Industry

- In 1963, book industry sales were $1.68 billion for 25,784 titles. In 1993, total book sales reached $16.1 billion with an average of 50,000 titles.
- The average hardback book cost $6.50 in 1963 compared with $22.50 in 1993.
- In 1992, eleven publishers captured 66 percent of the market. Small to medium-sized publishers claimed about 12.5 percent of the market.
- In 1994, children's publishing accounted for about 6 percent of the market with twelve publishing companies controlling 78 percent of the market.
- 100 million CD-ROM disks were manufactured worldwide in 1993. In the same year, U.S. consumers spent $172 million on CD-ROM titles. Publishers expect sales of $319 million in 1994.
- Women purchase 70 percent of all books sold, including 46 percent of all paperbacks.
- Men buy 16 times as many CD-ROM products as women.
- The average production cost of a hardback book ranges from $20,000 with mid-sized publishers to $50,000 with giant publishers.
- Eighty percent of all books published fail to earn back the advance given to their authors.
- Approximately 20,000 publishers produce most of the books published in the United States. Practically speaking, 40–50 could be considered major publishers.

while dining at exclusive New York restaurants. "There was no room!" Mary Alice Kier told the audience. "Manuscripts were stacked on every desk, table, and chair."

Northwest literary agent Natasha Kern estimates that she receives about 3000 query letters each year in addition to manuscripts. (A query letter describes a book idea and asks agents or editors if they would like to see more.) East-coast literary agent Denise Marcil receives about 100 letters each week. By volume of correspondence alone, agents and editors must read shorter forms—queries or proposals—and be selective about reading entire manuscripts.

The sheer quantity of manuscripts present a logistical problem for both agents and editors. They have no choice but to reject 99 percent of what they receive. This creates a competitive environment where agents and editors must choose the most well-written proposals. Despite this, don't assume that you've got about as much chance of gaining an agent or editor as winning the lottery. Only a small fraction of those who submit manuscripts understand the importance of using a proposal or know how to write one. This book will give you a critically important edge on the competition. Chapters one through thirteen explain how to write a salable proposal, and chapters fourteen and fifteen discuss agents, editors, and marketing.

Definition and Purpose of a Book Proposal

A book proposal is a marketing tool used to describe your book idea and sell it to a publisher. Virtually all nonfiction books are sold by proposal. It serves as the conventional means of communication between writer and agent/editor. In addition, it serves as a powerful aid to you, the writer, by helping you refine ideas, clarify organization, and speed the eventual writing of your book. Through the book proposal, you also address serious marketing questions for your publisher and present sample chapters from the actual book. In summary, a proposal accomplishes the following tasks:

- Presents the subject of your book;
- Introduces your qualifications for writing it;
- Analyzes the market, i.e. the audience;
- Compares your book to similar books already published;
- Offers ideas about how you'll help promote your book;
- Explains details about length, delivery, and format;
- Contains a detailed outline of your book;
- Includes sample chapters; and
- Inserts supportive documents that further sell the book or yourself as its author.

Parts of a Proposal

To fulfill its many purposes, the proposal has evolved into a document with as many corresponding sections. Although no industry standard has yet been set for the titles of these sections or for their order, most agents and editors prefer using headings and an arrangement that correspond to the following:

Title Page
The Concept Statement
Proposal Table of Contents
About the Book
About the Author
About the Market
About the Competition
Production Details
About Promotion
Table of Contents
Chapter Summaries
Sample Chapters
The Appendix

With the exception of the sample chapters, a proposal might be as short as ten pages or as long as forty, depending upon the complexity of the book and the thoroughness of the writer. In this book, you'll learn how to write each section by following an organization that I call "writer-up" versus "agent/editor down." This means that the chapters in this book are presented according to how you, the writer, will be able to most easily construct your proposal. Later, you'll assemble the proposal in the order shown above for agent/editor reading.

Why Not Send a Finished Manuscript?

Many times each year, I receive calls from writers who have completed their manuscripts and now feel ready for marketing and publication. You can imagine their surprise and disappointment when I inform them that agents and editors will not accept completed manuscripts. When agents or editors do receive completed books in lieu of proposals, they cannot put them into the usual channels for making a sale, because they have no answers to questions of marketing, competition, and production. Usually, they'll send you a form rejection letter and the manuscript—if you enclose return postage. If you're lucky, an agent/editor will read some of your book and send back a letter encouraging you to write a proposal.

Literary agents, who sell books to publishers on behalf of writers, are generally the first readers of a proposal. The proposal acts as the only vehicle of sale for your nonfiction book and, eventually, the proposal will be scrutinized by editors, a production person, sales representative, publicity and promotions person, and possibly a publisher/owner. This group is called the editorial review committee. If all parties agree on your book's merit, then you'll be offered a contract.

Before you throw up your arms and declare, "This looks too complex," let me assure you that writing a proposal is no more difficult than putting together a term paper, and it's a lot easier, by the way, than writing an entire manuscript. Of necessity, the proposal has many parts that serve the many people who use it to make important marketing and publishing decisions. After all, you're asking someone to invest tens of thousands of their dollars in your idea. Believe me, they'll want detailed information before they make a decision.

Who Reads Your Proposal?

Connecting books with publishers takes place through the efforts of:

- Literary agents;
- Acquisitions editors;
- Editorial committees; and
- Book packagers.

The pros and cons of marketing your proposal to an agent or editor are detailed in chapter fourteen. However, the descriptions that follow should give you some basic information about these different channels.

LITERARY AGENTS

Literary agents are to writers and editors what real-estate agents are to home sellers and buyers. Like most real-estate agents, literary agents work for the seller; that is, the writer. Literary agents get paid only when they sell your book to a publishing house. Like most real-estate agents, they work on commission. Literary agents typically receive 15 percent on your book's advance and royalties, while you get the remainder of the advance and later royalties.

An advance is money you receive upon signing a contract to complete writing the book. An advance is like borrowing money until pay day; it's money against revenues when your book sells. It's based in part on a formula: the number of books in the print run multiplied by the retail price of the book multiplied by the author's royalty rate (anywhere from about 5 percent for a mass market paperback to about 12 percent for hardback). Fortunately, if your book takes a loss, you do not normally have to repay the advance. Publishers consider an advance as an investment in you and in future works. Royalties are monies you make from the sale of your book, minus the advance.

Literary agents now sell about 90 percent of all published books. As the middle person in the chain from writer to publisher, literary agents select the most promising book ideas, offer editorial advice for polishing a manuscript, and take over the task of marketing your proposal to editors. An agent also acts as your cheerleader to editors and as your buffer from harsh words of rejection. Agents haggle with offers and know which parts of the publishing contract are negotiable. They iron out communications between authors and publishing personnel, recommend publicists, advise on career development, and sell your book to other countries and to Hollywood.

In other words, literary agents have skills that make them indispensable to most authors. And to editors. During the last decade the publishing industry suffered downsizing due to takeovers by conglomerates, changes in management, and recessionary economics. As a result, publishers began to rely more and more upon literary agents to *find* books for them. Given the many manuscripts received by publishing offices, this made good business sense: less need for editorial assistants, less expense, and more efficiency by trusting reliable agents to recommend manuscripts.

Even though so many books are sold through literary agents, they are not the best route for sale of specialized or regional books. In fact, with any book you may choose to directly query editors at publishing houses.

ACQUISITIONS EDITORS

Acquisitions editors, whether fulltime or freelance, are employees of publishers. They are the ones who communicate with agents and writers and make the initial decision about whether to accept or reject your proposal.

Although some of the largest publishers now consider only proposals submitted by agents, many—if not most—of this continent's publishers still review query letters sent directly by writers. If the query piques their interest, these editors will request and seriously consider your proposal. At small, or even mid-sized publishers, the acquisitions editor may also be part or full owner of the company. In some cases, this editor has 100 percent control over which books get published. At larger houses, the decision usually falls to the editorial committee.

EDITORIAL COMMITTEE

Before this proposal book found a home with Blue Heron Publishing, I had tried marketing it to larger publishers. An acquisitions editor at St. Martin's Press liked my proposal well enough to present it to his company's editorial committee—twice. In both attempts, his desire to take on the book was overruled. The sales department prevailed.

At larger houses, capturing the interest of the editor assigned to your kind of book is *only* the first step, although an important one. In fact, a large publisher may have many editors, each vying for his or her favorite proposals to fill the slots in an upcoming list. List refers to the lineup of books selected for a next catalog. Typically, a proposal must find acceptance from editorial committee members representing sales, promotion, production, and editing. Even the publisher/owner may express a view. This team must believe your book is worthy and would sell well before an editor calls you or your agent with an offer. This may seem as difficult as finding the proverbial needle in the haystack—to them and you—but books of all kinds and quality pass through this process every day.

In contrast, Blue Heron co-publisher Dennis Stovall reviewed my proposal with his wife and co-publisher Linny Stovall. They decided this book would be a good addition to their list. Some smaller publishers will check with their printer, graphic artist, and publicity manager to help determine if a book is profitable, but the entire decision about whether to publish a particular book rests with the publisher/owner.

BOOK PACKAGERS

Also referred to as book developers, book packagers are a hybrid of book publishers and agents. Only becoming a presence on this continent since the seventies, book packagers provide publishers with services ranging from artists, photographers, and writers to completely edited and finished books. Like subcontractors, they take some of the load off publishers, although they may also approach publishers with book proposals.

The main advantage of book packagers to nonfiction book writers is the opportunity packagers offer for entry into publishing if other avenues close. Packagers have editors who take time to work with and train writers. They also use writers-for-hire who may never receive direct credit for books they write, yet gain invaluable experience and pay. Book packagers may purchase your book outright, providing no royalties, or they may offer you an advance and royalties.

Some book packagers produce only a handful of books each year; others churn out as many as several hundred. Among the approximate 150 book packagers, only a dozen or so invite queries from writers about book projects. If interested, they will request a proposal. Most of the time, packagers contact writers they know or have referred to them. Since their use of writers varies so widely, you can learn more about this johnny-come-lately to publishing by reading about book packagers in *Writer's Market* and *Literary Market Place.*

Overview of the Publishing Industry

With approximately 20,000 publishers to select from, one of your tasks is figuring out which publisher is right for your project. As Sidebar 1-2 shows, one quarter of the publishers, or about 5000, do most of the publishing. However, that number still creates a quandary over where your book belongs.

To narrow this field, you must match your subject and approach with your targeted audience and with the right size and type of publisher. By size, you can categorize your options into large—and everybody else. A conglomerate, like Simon & Schuster, or Bantam-Doubleday-Dell resembles an octopus. Each arm represents publishing houses or divisions, called imprints. About eight of these giants dominate nearly 80 percent of all publishing.

The remaining 20 percent include mid-to small-sized publishers—including regional publishers, university publishers, independent small press, nonprofit publishers, and presses dedicated to extremely narrow market niches.

One of your tasks will be to figure out whether your book fits the demands of a conglomerate or if it better meets the criteria for a smaller or

Sidebar 1-2
Overview of the Publishing Industry

Type of Publisher	* Number of Publishers
General trade books, hardcover	850
General trade books, paperback	1200
Mass-market paperback	200
Juvenile and young adult	380
University and scholarly presses	900
Foreign language and bilingual	200
Association presses	100
Small presses	200
Fine editions	100
Books on cassettes	160
Audiovisual materials	150
Video cassettes	220
Belles lettres	15
CD-ROM electronic books	39
Databases	120
Micropublishers	100
TOTAL	4934

These publishers produce most of the 50,000 titles published on the average each year. Information taken from 1994 Literary Market Place.

specialty publisher. The proposal process is designed to lead you to this answer.

Writing for the Twenty-first Century

The use of the personal computer created a revolution in publishing that will send reverberations into the next century. Since its widespread introduction into our culture in the 1980s, the "PC" is now as much a fixture in most homes and businesses as the television or telephone.

The Computer Age has brought good news and bad news. For authors, the good news is that more channels of publishing have opened and are still being defined. Electronic publishing was unheard of twenty years ago. As Sidebar 1-1 indicated, sales of CD-ROM titles alone is nothing short of phenomenal. The only agreement among publishing professionals is that we're only seeing the beginning of electronic publishing.

As a global culture, we want to know more about our world, including its new inventions and its old ways. And, we want our information instantly. Demand is higher than ever for the printed word, and, now, the electronic word.

The bad news is that everyone is a writer. Agents and editors complain about the log jam of manuscripts. Word processing makes it possible to create multiple copies of a manuscript with no more than a few taps on the keyboard. One publishing expert estimates that half a million manuscripts are circulating at any given time in search of publication.

Regardless of whether, to paraphrase Dickens, now is the best of times or the worst of times, this book's "writer-up" organization will help lead you toward your goal of a book contract. If you follow the steps in this book, you'll have a superbly organized, professionally written, and marketable nonfiction book proposal.

The first step toward that goal is evaluating and refining your idea.

CHAPTER TWO

Evaluating and Refining Your Ideas: Preparing to Write Your Book

Chapter Goal: To refine your book idea—testing its worthiness and slanting it for greater salability.

Recognizing your expertise and enthusiasm for a particular subject, well-meaning people may have told you, "You should write a book." It's great to have their support, but don't take their encouragement as a signal to quit your day job, dash off a quick book, and bank on royalty checks rolling in.

The biggest mistake writers make is to start writing too soon, before they've done any planning or organization or additional research. That process begins with

> Books require planning. This is always true of good books, books that endure and sell year after year.

deeper examination of your idea, of its merits and marketability, and of your writing skill.

Ideas Agents and Editors Seek

If you had a crystal ball, you would know exactly what agents, editors, and the inscrutable public are looking for. Since you don't, you'll need to study the forecast guides they use. *Publishers Weekly* is *the* trade journal of the industry. You'll become familiar with the major players, publishers, and their policies. By the time you read six months' to a year's worth of this magazine, including the fat fall and spring issues, you'll know what's selling now and what will be on the shelves in the immediate future. You'll identify trends, spot fads, and figure out which literary waves have already crested. You'll even begin to see who sells what to whom.

Literary agents and editors keep attuned to timing, to what's hitting the market now, as well as to what is scheduled to come out. For books on

> Remember, it usually takes a year or more to complete a proposal, find an agent, and sell your book to a publisher.

anniversaries of historical events, such as 50 years after WWII or the upcoming 200-year celebration of Lewis & Clark's trek across the Oregon Trail to the Pacific Ocean, you must plan further ahead than publishers who make acquisitions years in advance. Agents and editors are "idea people" and book lovers. They yearn to find the next book that will top the bestseller list.

Read *Publishers Weekly, The New York Times Book Review, The Small Press Review* and what's written in your field. Stay abreast of current trends, cultural shifts, and new discoveries. The presentation of your idea in the form of a proposal *must* excite an agent, who in turn *must* excite an editor, who in turn *must* excite everyone else on the editorial committee. After publication, the sales representative *must* like your book better than most of the other titles he represents, becoming so excited that he makes his retailers decide to carry it and talk it up to their customers. At each step, everyone should be excited about the market potential of your book, even if they themselves have no interest in its specific content, whether that be small Victorian gardens, how to parent teens, or discovering Iowa on foot. Literary agent Denise Marcil said it well: "The best writing is from the heart. When a writer is truly excited about a topic, I get excited and say, 'Wow!'"

Evaluating Your Idea

Evaluating and refining your book idea constitutes one of the most important steps in the success of your book project. The more you examine and

> Consider your book idea as carefully as you would buying a house or car.

dissect your idea before beginning your proposal, the more time you will save and the fewer headaches you will suffer.

PASSING THE PERSONAL TEST

Before you analyze the marketplace, I believe your book idea must pass a personal test—intellectually, emotionally, and spiritually. In particular, ask yourself the following questions. Be honest and make sure you are satisfied with your answers.

- Are you enthusiastic enough about this idea to stick with it for, say, five years, from conception through publication to promotion?
- Are you qualified (or could you become qualified) to write this book?
- Does writing this book match your long-term career goals? Can you describe how publication of this book will make a difference in how you view yourself and how you are viewed by others whose opinions you respect?
- Are you willing to learn how to write for publication?

Can You Stick With it?

I have met people who believe they *should* write a book on a particular subject, whether or not they want to. Often, they believe it would be a good career move, even though their hearts aren't in it. Some let themselves become strong-armed by a well-meaning spouse or friend. Don't get caught in that trap. Your time and life energy are too precious not to write about what you enjoy and about subjects that excite you. After all, if you're not excited yourself, how can you hope to interest an agent?

Are You Qualified?

Ask yourself if you are truly qualified to write a book on your subject. If not, could you (or would you take the time to) develop the necessary credentials? In our culture, only doctors are permitted by law to give medical advice. Only attorneys can practice law. Outside of licensure and diplomas, our culture still demands substantial credentials before conferring the mantle of "authority." If your car broke down, you would no more take it to your licensed hair stylist than you would let your dealer-certified mechanic style your hair.

In lieu of earning the credentials of a doctor, lawyer, mechanic, or stylist, you can be the writer half of a writer/expert team. To pursue this route, you must demonstrate professional writing and interview skills and be willing to immerse yourself in the knowledge and language of your expert's field. In essence, you would have to become a professional in two fields—the expert's and in writing. It goes without saying that both writer and expert should sign an agreement about division of labor

15

and money for the creation of the proposal and book, as well as for its promotion.

As an alternative to teaming up with an expert, you can also research, write, and publish articles in academic, technical, or professional areas. Many freelance writers make a living by studying the journals and conference papers, in science, for instance, and translating them into articles and books for the general public. Over time, you can build a reputation as lay expert, and then write a proposal and book.

We've been discussing "the professions and the trades," but developing credentials (or teaming up with an expert) applies to nonprofessional areas as well. For instance, one would think that preparing three meals a day for all your adult life would stand as sufficient qualifications to write cookbooks. Before you sit down to whip up a cookbook proposal, I'd want to know if you've published articles on cooking. No? Taught cooking classes? No? Starred in a local TV cooking show? I didn't think so. Before you can share your secret sauce with the world, you've got to convince agents and editors that you know what you're talking about. Testimonials from sated family members are not enough.

Does Your Book Idea Match Your Long-term Career Goals?

Last of all, consider the career implications of publishing the book you have in mind. You may develop a following, become known or better known, after you publish a book. Some writers publish books in order to create new careers. For instance, a book may be used to launch a speaking tour, which then allows a person to become a consultant. In general, editors will assume you want to write a book similar to your first in order to capitalize on name recognition. Do I have other books in mind on writing? You bet.

Think about what shape you'd like your life and career as a writer to take in five years, ten years, and beyond. Make sure you would be proud to have a particular book as your legacy to the world. Publishing a book grants you an instant mantle of authority—like Dr. Spock or Rachel Carson. Do you want to be remembered by your present book idea?

You must have clear and positive answers to these questions of personal impact. If you're still on solid ground with your book idea, go on and ask yourself whether you're ready to refine, or even develop, the writing skills you'll need to go the distance.

Are You Willing to Learn How to Write for Publication?

Proposals showcase writing, and your writing must show well. Writing for publication is vastly different from writing essays about "My Summer Vacation" or "Analysis of the Symbolism in Hemingway's *The Old Man and the Sea*" for a term paper. Most writers require specialized training to write successful proposals and books. The examples drawn from proposals in this book reveal the kind of professional writing and marketing style common to proposals.

Roger Devine, former assistant trade books editor with Viking/Penguin USA, quoted in a *Writer's Digest* article, stated: "Ninety-eight percent of the things that come to me are written by people who can't write." Echoing this sentiment, New York literary agent Denise Marcil cites poor grammar, punctuation, and prose as the most annoying weaknesses in proposals submitted to her.

In this book's Resource Directory, I've listed a few books and correspondence courses for review of freelance writing technique.

> Read several books on freelance writing to learn the techniques of writing for publication.

As used in this book, "writing for publication" does not mean writing textbooks or journal articles. Writers with advanced degrees or years spent in professional or highly technical fields—such as professors, doctors, therapists, computer buffs, scientists—often speak and write in three-to-five-syllable words or in technical jargon. If you are one of the "higher-educationally impaired," you may have to unlearn high diction and techno-speak in order to communicate to a general reader. Psychologist Marilyn Barrett, author of *Creating Eden: The Garden as a Healing Space*, based her book on her Ph.D. thesis. She worked through several revisions of her proposal with a professional editor until she "recovered her natural voice."

PASSING A PUBLISHER'S TEST

It's important to sensitize yourself to the publishing perspective shared by agents and editors. They are constantly on the lookout for great ideas and new trends. The four basic criteria you must fulfill with any nonfiction book are to:

- Fill a void;
- Make a contribution;

- Offer something different or better; and
- Meet the demands of the times.

Fill a Void

When no book has yet been published in an area where there is public interest or need, there is an opportunity for a writer to "fill a void." When Dr. Darald A. Treffert wrote his proposal on the "savant syndrome," he found no book on the subject written for the lay public. He filled the void with *Extraordinary People*. The key that makes a publisher willing to risk publication of a never-been-done book is the combination of heightened public interest and solid author credentials.

Make a Contribution

When other authors have already written in your subject area, but you have something substantive to add to the field, you have an opportunity to make a contribution. Often, making a contribution goes hand in hand with supplying a book that is different or better and timely—the next two criteria. Some agents and editors feel a personal responsibility to help into print those book ideas that serve humanity, that make a contribution in a social or moral way. Often, these works make little money, and yet an agent or publishing company that champions these books will go the distance to see that they get published.

Offer Something Different or Better

While your book may not speak for a previously disenfranchised group or tap into a social problem, it should offer something different or better. When I first conceived the idea for this book, for instance, only one other book on proposals served the public. Unhappy with its limitations I set out to produce a book that was both different and better.

Our global culture has been oriented around a virtually insatiable thirst for information-supplying books and how-tos. As George Witte, an editor with St. Martin's Press said at a writer's conference, "There are lots of books that are not works of genius but provide solid information." As you read through the proposal examples in this book, you'll see that nearly every author supplies the criteria of different or better.

Meet the Demands of the Times

The sixty-four-thousand-dollar question in publishing is, "Why this book? Why now?" In a real sense, timing is everything. Books sell not just because they prove to be different or better, or even because they fill a void or make a contribution. If the timing isn't right, none of these criteria particularly matter. Your book must fulfill the demands of the times, the ever-changing interests and needs of the public. Scientist Linda Jean Shepherd might not have been able to sell her book, *Lifting the Veil: The Feminine Face of Science* in, say, the fifties. But it was precisely the right book to meet the demands of the nineties.

In contrast, space engineer Ralph Nansen has had a hard time selling his revolutionary book, *The Fourth Era: Energy From Space.* He may be the most qualified person in the country to know whether our technology could reasonably and economically shift to his solar-energy plan, yet the editorial feedback he's received indicates that he may be ahead of the demands of the times.

In an entirely different sense of "the demands of the times," some authors intentionally capitalize on the short-lived fads of popular culture and big events. Have you ever noticed how quickly books hit the stands following a major disaster, such as a hurricane, flood, or earthquake? Not to mention books on high-profile criminal proceedings and celebrities. Some writers make a comfortable living just by seizing the element of timing.

Not only writers, but agents and publishers also keep apprised of long-range anniversaries of historical events and begin planning books for them years in advance. If you want to sell a book about the twentieth anniversary of the 1980 eruption of Mt. St. Helens, write that proposal in 1995 or 1996.

Many other books are perennials, not heavily affected by time, except when their information becomes dated. When I asked several publishing professionals what kinds of books they considered as perennials, they said: childcare/parenting, personal finance/planning, pet care, home how-to, personal health/fitness, entrepreneurial, pop culture, how-tos and cooking, to name a few. Your best barometer for what's selling now and in the near future is the trade journal of publishing, *Publishers Weekly.*

Like the labs of *Consumer Reports*, Sidebar 2-1 will help you measure how well your idea will stand up to the demands of an editorial review committee before you commit to a proposal and book.

Sidebar 2-1

Editorial Review Committee's Most Common Reasons for Rejection of a Proposal

1. It sounds like a magazine article.

   You may have narrowed the subject too much, researched inadequately, or chosen too superficial a topic.

2. It's already been done.

   Angels, for instance. Other topics that have run their course and would be hard to get published include the giant recovery market, including the treatment of alcohol and drug addiction, codependent relationships, etc. To avoid a rehashing of topics already covered, research what's been written in your area, and check *Books in Print* and *Forthcoming Books in Print* to anticipate the market.

3. It's never been done.

   This reason for rejection means that the editors don't see a market for your book. They believe the public either wouldn't be interested in your new topic or would have to be educated to create a desire to buy your book. If you tend to ride the leading edge in your field, then write and publish articles first, in order to prepare the world for your new ideas.

4. Topics like that don't sell.

   Publishing has ingrained prejudices. Cat books sell; dog books don't (Never mind the bestseller, *The Secret Life of Dogs*). Baseball books sell; football books don't. World War II books sell; unknown authors' life stories don't. If you intend to overcome these biases, which are based on bottom-line profits, then you have extra work to do. You must have a well-developed slant and prove why your book will sell.

5. There's too much competition.

   Perhaps another publisher has a similar book coming out—an insider fact you and your agent may not know. Perhaps they've just received six proposals on the opossums and other marsupials. Agents and editors alike share their amazement in the synchronous phenomenon of receiving proposals for books on the same subject in a relatively brief time period. We do all seem to be swimming in the same sea of shared thought. Publishing goes in waves. Again, the remedy to entering an overly competitive field is to keep an eye on *Books in Print* and *Publishers Weekly*.

6. It's too expensive to produce.

So what if you've spent the last ten years writing the definitive tome on forest slugs. Nine hundred pages is too long and the color plates for 50 photographs will break all budgets. You'll either have to find a publisher with deeper pockets or adjust your ideas.

Refining Your Idea

You can't adequately refine an idea for a book without taking into consideration a market. Make sure you can answer these three marketplace questions:

- Who is my reader?
- How many readers could my book have?
- How can I slant my idea to attract my readers?

WHO IS MY READER?

Although you'll be asked to go into greater detail about your potential reader for the proposal section "About the Market," to refine your idea further, create a cameo of your intended readers. Who are they? What gender and age group would be most interested in your idea? What interests or professions do your targeted readers hold?

If you fail to ask and answer these questions early on, you may make a big mistake. Howard, a psychologist, decided he wanted to write a self-help book for the mass market. In one sense, Howard had defined his audience, because *mass* means everybody. However, within a few paragraphs, his sentences grew top-heavy with multisyllabic words, and his technical jargon overrode his message as he made lengthy detours into abstraction. In short, he ceased to communicate with his audience. Readers of self-help books want immediately useful ideas to apply to their lives, and the ideas must be reasonably simple. Howard also had another problem in his early draft: his examples inadvertently featured women in a poor light.

Keep in mind the amazing statistic that women purchase some 70 percent of all books and 46 percent of all paperbacks.

Another one of my students described a book idea based on her homespun solutions to raising children from birth to eighteen. Since I have two children, one teen and one preteen, I fit the profile of one of her potential readers. So far, so good. But, after a brief review, I knew I'd never buy her book. Nor would an agent, editor, or, I believe, any parent. Why? Her idea covered too great a scope for her targeted readers' needs or interests. I no longer need to learn how to handle the trying twos, toilet training, or bedtimes. Not anymore. Instead, I need advice on piloting my teenager through high-school homework, and on keeping both kids away from negative peer influences. The author's scope was simply too great.

In contrast to these two examples, by the time school counselor Dean Walker brought his proposal to my critique group, he had already narrowed his idea. This was evident by his working title: *Organic Parenting: Raising Real People Through the Art of Human Relating, Birth to Six*. Although his title seemed cumbersome, it did reflect careful thinking about his audience, parents of younger children. His distinction of "organic parenting"

Discuss your book idea with booksellers, librarians, and potential readers to ensure that the scope of your idea is appropriate.

also targeted a particular readership, parents whose values probably lean toward organic foods and whole-earth lifestyles.

HOW MANY READERS COULD MY BOOK HAVE?

Estimate the size of your market. Talk with bookstore owners or managers and listen to their answers. Ask if they'd expect your book to be published by a small, regional, or specialty publisher, by a mid-sized publisher, or by a large publisher. If a bookseller's answers are clear, focused, and immediate, you're probably on track. Your idea is clear and communicates well. If the person you talk with hesitates, puzzles over your idea, and gives you vague answers, take that response as a signal to spend more time thinking about what you want to write and who will want to read it. Also pay attention to these retailers' nonverbal responses; gauge how much excitement your idea generates.

Knowing the size of your market will allow you to make reasonable claims in your proposal and it will save you time in marketing it to the right publishers or agents. For example, this book on proposals is a specialized book. I'm unlikely to see this book on the *New York Times* bestsellers list. Only readers interested in writing nonfiction book proposals will pick up a how-to book on this subject.

HOW CAN I SLANT MY IDEA TO ATTRACT MY READERS?

One afternoon I received a call from a consummate gardener with the title of Master Gardener. She had recently moved from the Northeast

> Ask a bookseller where your book might be shelved—to profile your intended readers, to estimate the size of your market, and to see which publishers are already interested in your subject.

to my part of the world, the Northwest. After telling me about her credentials, which were substantial enough to write a book, she said, "I want to write a book on gardening." We talked further and I expected her to become more specific in her description of her book idea. Instead, she repeated, "Just on gardening."

She needed to prune her idea, to narrow its scope. Even though she could define her reader—gardeners—and could guess at the size of her potential market—she would never be able to write a proposal on "gardening" and sell it. Bookstore shelves sag under the weight of gardening books. Entire books have been written on roses, composting, or organic control of pests. Even so, the broad subject is a perennial, excuse the pun. Room exists for one more book; in fact, there's room for bushels more. However, because so much has already been written on the gardening, new books need a well-focused slant. They need to be narrowed to a smaller scope and to niches not already filled, such as "Postage stamp gardening for college dorm rooms," or "Dashboard gardening for the fulltime RVer."

Sometimes students and clients don't understand what I mean by narrowing an idea. It does evoke the idea of ending up with less. Yet in the book world, less usually means more. The best way to narrow your idea is to understand *slant*.

Slant means the focus of your subject or the angle you take in presenting it. Selecting a slant makes your book unique and gives it a sales angle. Slant establishes bias and "colors" an idea throughout, from title to chapter content. Imagine a beautiful sunset written about, first, for meteorologists and, second, for tourists. It's not just the slant of the suns rays that are important, but the perspective from which you write about them. In many ways, slant refines the notion of audience as much as subject.

Clarity of subject is by far the most important feature of your book's concept. If you have ever started a business or searched for a service by name, you will understand the need for a descriptive name rather than a cute one. Until name recognition, i.e. McDonalds or Levis, can sell your product or service, it's generally best to choose a business name like Magic Carpet Cleaning rather than Sam's Service Specialties. What specialty? What service? Who's Sam?

The same holds true for marketing your book. It's better to err on the side of plain description than to miss the mark with a fancy title or approach that reveals nothing of your book's contents. Consider these actual book titles: *The Prostate Book* or *Beachcomber's Guide to Florida Marine Life*. Descriptive and clear. In coauthor Carolyn Cotter's first draft of a proposal on psychophysiologist, George H. Green's model for countering manipulation, they titled the book, *Don't Even Try!* What does that mean? Give up? By the time she sent it out for agent consideration, it bore the title, *Earn Your Verbal Black Belt* with a descriptive subtitle. Personally, I preferred this title to the one eventually used, because it reflected the metaphor of the martial arts (a part of the book's actual content). Needless to say, I couldn't argue with the clear title selected by Elizabeth Beier, Green and Cotter's editor at Berkley Publishing Group: *Stop Being Manipulated*.

Titles offer an important reflection of slant. It may take you many tries and many months to find a title you are happy with, but start your thinking processes with a working title that reflects a slant. It's crucial to your idea's success to present your subject matter in a special way.

> You have to end up with so strong an idea that it can stand up to intense editorial scrutiny.

In her book entitled, *How to Write Irresistible Query Letters*, Lisa Collier Cool identifies over a dozen slants. I've listed the most common slants and given examples from recently published books in Sidebar 2-2 that follows. For instructional purposes, I've followed each example of an actual book

The Most Common Slants to Capture Reader Attention

Below, you'll find two examples in each category. The first is a published book. The last is an imaginary title as if I were brainstorming for a slant on a book about "cats."

- NEW—what's never been done before, the cutting edge. Example: *New French Thought: Political Philosophy* (Mark Lilla); or *New Cat Breeds*.
- MONEY—any allusion to the buck attracts attention. Example: *Big Profits from Small Stocks* (Samuel Case); or *Million-Dollar Cats*.
- SEXY—either direct reference or sexual innuendo uses sex as a sales slant. Example: *Nuts! The Battle of the Bulge* (Goldstein, Dillon, & Wenger); or *Furry Bedwarmers: The Cat in Your Life*.
- CONFIDENTIAL—secrets, inside accounts, behind the scenes all reflect this slant. Example: *Secrets of Fat-Free Baking* (Sandra Woodruff); or *Behind Bars: The Untold Story of Impounded Cats*.
- PROMISES—this slant offers the moon and better deliver. Example: *Eat More, Weigh Less* (Dean Ornish, M.D.); or *Cats That Can Change Your Life*.
- CALL-OF-THE-WILD—meant to arouse brainstem feelings of fight or flight, this slant gets adrenaline rushing. Example: *Jungle Rules: How to be a Tiger in Business* (Imlay and Hamilton); or *Catting Around: Stalking Big Cat Home Videos*.
- INTIMIDATION—when you want to make your reader afraid, this slant is the one to use. Example: *Outrageous Practices: The Alarming Truth About How Medicine Mistreats Women* (Laurence and Weinhouse); or *An Endangered Species: Big Cats Fall to Small-Armed Men*.
- NUMBERS—whether the number refers to time, pounds, age, or anything else, it is a classic slant. Example: *The 7 Habits of Highly Effective People* (Stephen R. Covey); or *Ten Ideal Vacations for Kitty*.
- LOCATION—any idea that implies place, by geography or smaller location, reflects this slant. Example: *In the Kitchen with Rosie* (Rosie Daley); or *Bedroom Designs for Catting Around*.
- AMAZING FACTS—a slant that gives you a believe-it-or-not feeling or elicits amazement. Example: *Remarkable Discoveries!*

(Frank Ashall); or *The Cat Who Dogpaddled the Channel.*

- SUPERLATIVES—any title that involves extremes, such as worst, best, longest, shortest, richest, poorest, etc. Example: *The Greatest Team of All Time* (Acocella and Dewey); or *The Sleepiest Cats in the World.*
- REVERSALS—minority viewpoints or an opposite stance from the prevailing orientation on a subject. Example: *Roughing It Easy* (on camping by Dian Thomas); or, *Seeing-Eye Cats.*
- TRAVEL—Rather than location, or in addition to it, the travel slant makes clear the out-and-about orientation of the book. Example: *A Cat Abroad: The Further Adventures of Norton, The Cat Who Went to Paris, and His Human* (Peter Gethers)—I didn't make this one up; or *Cruises Cats Love.*
- HUMOR—a humorous slant on an idea is enough to provide the sharp focus that every subject demands. Example: *I Purr, Therefore I Am: Never Before Collected Observations on All Things Cat* (compiled by Merrit Malloy)—I didn't make this one up either; or *Paw-Print Picassos: Your Cat as Artist.*

with one based on the idea of writing a book about "cats." Take your narrowed book concept and check it against the list of slants. Refine your idea by rewriting it with a slant.

> Select a slant for your idea, and reflect it in your book's working title, and then throughout your proposal.

To explore the full possibilities of a slant for your idea, write a title for your book using each slant.

As you can see from the examples of slants, just taking the simple (and broad) category of "cats" allowed me to create a narrowed subject with diverse avenues of sales appeal.

Your publisher may later change your working title into a more descriptive one. Never forget, however, that you'll make your first sell to a sophisticated buyer—an agent and editor. Because I was involved in directly presenting Green and Cotter's book to several agents, I watched them perk up when they heard the working title, *Earn Your Verbal Black Belt.* I'm not sure they would have been equally interested in *Stop Being Manipulated,* yet this may better reach the book's mass-market readership.

It takes time to arrive at a solid book idea. Preliminary research will help you continue to evaluate and refine your idea. Research will also form the foundation for drafting the first section of your proposal called "About the Competition."

> Refine your concept until it is broad enough for a book, but make the slant so different that your book will emerge as unique from all others.

Sidebar 2-3

Ten Questions to Answer Before Committing to a Book Project

1. Can you write well enough—with correct grammar, punctuation, and coherence? If the answer is *no*, are you willing to learn how to bring your writing up to standard?

2. Do you have sufficient enthusiasm for a project that may span years?

3. Are you qualified to write your book? Can you develop qualifications?

4. Will publication of your book satisfy your long-term career goals? Will you be proud of this book in years to come?

5. Is your book idea better than or different from other books already published on your subject?

6. What is the size of your market? Will your book appeal to a small, middle-sized, or large audience?

7. Do you have enough material for an entire book?

8. Does your subject have staying power? Will it reach beyond a current trend and sell copies in three, five, or ten years?

9. Does your idea spark enthusiasm? As you share it, do your friends, booksellers, and prospective readers become excited?

10. Is your slant fresh and interesting?

CHAPTER THREE

Research Made Easy:
What Data Will You Need?

Chapter Goal: To create a foundation for writing your proposal by recognizing and planning the necessary research.

When graduate students begin doctoral theses, they sometimes spend a year or more researching their subjects. Such research is the foundation for a successful proposal too, but some shortcuts will get you in and out of the library before you have to put another quarter in the parking meter.

To many people, research is an eight-letter bad word. Their negative experiences may have been based upon the laborious ways we formerly did research with stacks of index cards, piles of books, and mounds of photocopied paper. It is my intent to relieve your suffering by streamlining your task, first, by letting you know what kinds of research you'll need, and second, by introducing you to the most effective research tools available. Then, you can maximize results and minimize labor.

> Research is necessary and invaluable, but it need not be protracted and painful!

Overview of Research Requirements for the Proposal

Although it's likely that you'll do most research little by little as you develop your proposal, a comprehensive overview may help give you the "big picture" of your research needs. Sidebar 3-1 provides this overview.

Six Research Tools

I'm one of those individuals who loves research. Often, I become so fascinated with tidbits I find that I easily go off on tangents, nearly forgetting

Sidebar 3-1
Overview of Research Needs for Your Proposal

Proposal Section	Research Needed
The Concept Statement	ranges from no special research to some statistics or startling facts
About the Book	statistics, interesting facts, quotes from printed sources, quotes from experts and person-in-the-street, a solid background understanding of your book's idea, knowledge of most competitive books like yours, identification of your targeted reader
About the Author	a good memory
About the Market	statistics to document the demographics of your audience and the size of your market
About the Competition	*Books in Print, Cumulative Index,* and *Forthcoming Books in Print,* as well as books most similar to yours; trips to well-stocked bookstores and interviews with owners or managers
Production Details	permissions forms, individuals to endorse book and write a foreword, costs to complete book
About Promotion	books on marketing books
Table of Contents	books like yours to compare organization and style
Chapter Summaries	information that goes into each chapter
Sample Chapters	details—facts, statistics, information to write these chapters
The Appendix	magazines, journals, and newspapers for material related to your subject, personal archives for clips, flyers, public relations materials on you and your subject

my original goal. If you're already familiar with doing research, you may not need this section. However, if you're like most writers, you'll appreciate having the following six research tools, especially the first, to provide you with a clear direction.

- Reference librarians;
- Computerized on-line catalogs;
- Periodical directories;
- Databases;
- Authorities in your field; and
- Books in print and out of print.

REFERENCE LIBRARIANS

Viva librarians! They are a writer's greatest research resource. Librarians at college or university libraries will assist you with computerized searches for information, as well as with more traditional reference texts. Sometimes a writer will feel stymied, overwhelmed by the need to drum up statistics for the proposal sections that require them. Befriend a reference librarian. If you don't live close to a university library, reference librarians at your local public library remain "at your service," even for phone inquiries. Or use one of the excellent books on research listed in the Resource Directory.

> Gain maximum help from research librarians by fully informing them of your project and the information you need.

COMPUTERIZED ON-LINE CATALOGS

Most libraries have replaced traditional card catalogs, which show the books in inventory, with computerized catalogs. Using these, you or a librarian can track down books available at your library or branch libraries, searching by title, subject, author, or other key words. These simple-to-operate programs can give you descriptions of the contents of individual books, and help you find synonyms of your topic. Use these to cross-index your topic with related subjects.

On-line services produce great efficiency in preparation for writing "About the Competition." For this section, you'll be required to review other books similar to yours. But it won't be necessary to read every one of them. On-line references provide summaries of each book that help you eliminate those you don't need, and alert you to competitive books you should spend time reading from cover to cover.

For any book description you might use in your competition section, copy the library description as well as the library call numbers, such as the Dewey decimal numbers or Library of Congress numbers. File these for later reference so you don't need to repeat your initial search.

For the books you choose to cite, include the following:

- Author's name;
- Book title;
- Publisher;
- City of publication;
- Publication date;
- Number of pages; and
- Retail cost of hardback or paperback—if available.

PERIODICAL DIRECTORIES

Periodicals reflect the ever-changing fads of our culture more quickly than books do. One of the critical questions you must answer for an agent/ editor in "About the Book" is: "Why this idea; why now?" Magazine articles will tell you whether your idea is passe, in vogue, or just about to be "discovered." Magazines and newspapers also offer current statistics, facts, and quotable passages that add pizzazz to your concept statement, about the book, and marketing sections. Periodical directories list what has been published in the past few years in magazines, journals, and newspapers.

The *Reader's Guide to Periodical Literature* and other directories, (see Resource Directory), give an extensive index of trade, technical, religious, and college publications. They fill in gaps by providing indexed and abstracted descriptions of magazine and journal articles published on this continent and across the world.

DATABASES

Computer databases bring literally an entire planet of research to your fingertips. Think of a database as a library that specializes in a particular subject area. Reference librarians need only type the correct computer queries to discover the specific information you request in virtually every field of interest. Doing in-depth research has never been so quick or so comprehensive. Get to know how to research databases.

Some databases provide the full text of the publications you desire while others provide photocopies—for a fee. You decide. Art Spikol, a columnist with *Writers Digest Magazine* noted that "...database searching will...allow you to bring together disparate pieces of information that have probably never been brought together before." That's exciting, if not revolutionary.

Consult your librarian. Or, invest in a modem for your personal computer. A modem is a device that allows you to connect to a standard phone line to join a service that rents access to databases. In other words, you can "go to the libraries of the world" from your home computer. Most of the services charge a flat monthly rate and add additional fees for your telephone time. Most also offer access to dictionaries, encyclopedias, *Books in Print*, and newspapers.

> To save hours and days, call a reference librarian and set up an appointment. Let this research professional lead the way. You'll be gratified by the results.

From periodicals or databases, you should:

- Confirm that your book supplies a current need or fills a publishing void;
- Make sure that your subject offers enough substance for a book, enough slant to attract your readers; and
- Begin to define how your book will be different and better than existing books.

When you find good articles related to your book's subject, photocopy them and record bibliographic information. At a later date, you may wish to review articles again for quotes to use within your chapters or for verification of facts and statistics. You may also decide to include copies of some articles in your proposal's appendix to demonstrate the popularity of your topic.

AUTHORITIES IN YOUR FIELD

Plan to interview authorities on your book's subject for purposes of acquiring original, unpublished contributions to your book or proposal (with credit), and for recommendations of other books on your subject. Interviews with experts in your field can add information you won't find in publications.

BOOKS IN PRINT AND OUT OF PRINT

For your competition section, you need to know what is current on your subject, and perhaps, what has gone out of print. I'm convinced that a high percentage of writers conduct a search of the literature by going to their local bookstore and finding "nothing much." If you rely upon memory, if you research only your personal collection of books on your topic or those books in stock at a favorite bookstore, you risk writing a proposal that is too narrow and vague, has shallow development, and makes an inadequate comparison of your book with others.

This means searching beyond your local library and bookstore. You *must* check Bowker's *Books in Print* and *Forthcoming Books in Print*. If you want to write a nonfiction book

> Find out what's been published, and review those books most similar to yours for eventual use in your proposal's competition section.

for children, check *Children's Books in Print*. These are major reference books carried by every library and frequently updated. Many, if not most, libraries also have them available in a database accessible by the library computers. Another source for checking what's in and out of print is the on-line catalog I mentioned earlier.

These indexes are divided by subject, author, and title. The subject index allows you to directly check your topic. If necessary, ask your reference librarian to help you create a list of synonyms for cross-referencing. Find out what's been published in your subject area, paying close attention to those books most like your own.

If your research does not indicate a viable idea, your investment of time will have spared you rejection down the road. Preliminary research can reveal some of those

> One additional result of your research should be greater validation that you have a viable idea.

editorial reasons for rejection, such as "it's already been done," or "it sounds like a magazine article," or "it's never been done." If this turns out to be the case, you've saved yourself time, effort, and from disappointment.

Despite thorough research into the competition, what if your results are inconclusive, or you're simply unsure whether your idea is worth developing into a book? Perhaps you found dozens of books like yours, but still believe yours is significantly different. Or perhaps you couldn't find any truly comparable books in print, yet you believe you have a book the world needs or would enjoy. I'll address these uncertainties in the next chapter.

CHAPTER FOUR

About the Competition: What's Already in Print?

Chapter Goal: To compare and contrast your book to others, and write a powerful "About the Competition."

The Concept Statement
About the Book
About the Author
About the Market
• **About the Competition**
Production Details
About Promotion
Table of Contents
Chapter Summaries
Sample Chapters
The Appendix

Seeking publication is similar to selling a new product. You wouldn't think of ignoring competing models. Your buyer (in this case your publisher) would be foolish to offer you a contract without knowing the competition. It may surprise you, but competition for your book may actually be a good thing. In fact, finding other books in your field demonstrates public interest and prior publisher confidence.

Definition and Purpose

The profiles of competitive titles for your proposal are in the section called "About the Competition." Here, authors typically profile half-a-dozen to a dozen books most like their own. In each profile, list bibliographic information, summarize the competitor's book, then compare and contrast it with yours.

Although the competition section is usually the fifth section in a finished proposal, this book asks you to address it now, as part of the process of determining if your idea fills a publishing void and whether your book will make a contribution to the field. If you can't substantiate that, there's little point in making a heavy investment of time and energy in the proposal process.

You don't want to reinvent the wheel. Your research of competitive titles should validate your unique spin on your subject. Learning what the competition has already written will merely help you refine your idea, allowing you to further slant it for greater salability.

Like many of my clients, you may be surprised that it is the job of the writer, not the publisher, to profile the competition. However, realize that the entire proposal represents a market-research report, and that the burden of proof of your book's need rests with you. You're the party seeking financial backing.

Similar to selling any product, the sale of your book depends upon briefing the publisher about your competition and providing a convincing argument why your book is better or different or both—why your book represents the *zeitgeist*, the spirit of the times.

Your choice of books in "About the Competition" also tells the publisher where you see your book being shelved. For some books, their shelving locations are easy to determine. *Mothering Twins: From Hearing the News to Beyond the Terrible Twos* clearly belongs with books on family, parenting, or birthing (depending upon the volume and diversity in a bookstore). But where would you shelve *Creating Eden: The Garden as a Healing Space*? Gardening? Nature and ecology? Self-help? Where you position your book—by comparison to others—helps crystallize your vision of it and how it will be marketed.

Sample "About the Competition"

Because Rosemarie Ostler's subject, language, is narrow, her competition section on *The Hidden Life of Language* includes only three books. It is an excellent model, although variations will be introduced later in the chapter. See Sidebar 4-1. I've included one of her three comparisons and added some marginal comments.

Performing Background Research

Begin your search for books for your competition section by using the subject index to *Books in Print*. It gives short descriptions of books, includ-

---

Sidebar 4-1
Sample: About the Competition

Proposal	Comments

The subject of language is perennially popular. Periodically, there is a surge of interest, reflected in the appearance of new books. One such surge took place in the 1950s and early 1960s. Books for general audiences published in this period include...These books are still popular with library patrons, although they are very much out-of-date. The accumulation of knowledge that has occurred in linguistics in the last forty years is revolutionary. Reading these books is comparable to reading physics books that do not mention the theory of relativity. However, until recently, they have been the only options for the nonspecialist reader.

Reinforces popularity of subject and gives background of publishing.

Signals steady backlist potential (titles that are no longer new, have passed their sales peak but still sell predictably) and hints at need for updated info.

This year has seen another upswing of interest in linguistic publishing. Three books have appeared which target the same audience as *The Hidden Life of Language*. A review of these books shows that they differ from this book in significant ways. They are not as general or accessible, and do not

Emphasizes timeliness and a wave of public interest in language.

Begins case for her book as better and different.

---

ing bibliographic data. Because most writers discover more books than the six to twelve needed for their competition sections, you should:

- Eliminate dissimilar titles;
- Check recent out-of-print titles;

<table>
<tr><td>present the same type of material.</td><td></td></tr>
<tr><td>The book most comparable to this one is Steven Pinker's The Language Instinct: How the Mind Creates Language (Morrow, 1994, 494 pp, $23. HB).</td><td>Notes bibliographic data.</td></tr>
<tr><td>It too discusses the development of language in early humans and explains the distinction between people's intrinsic linguistic knowledge and the rules they learn from grammar books.</td><td>Shows similarities to her book.</td></tr>
<tr><td>However, it approaches these topics from a different vantage point. Pinker's specialty is cognitive psychology. He describes language from the perspective of developmental psychology and neurolinguistics. He concentrates almost entirely on these aspects of language and on an explanation of current</td><td>Shows differences from her book.

Summarizes competitor; notice the omission of repetition of any title other than hers.</td></tr>
<tr><td>linguistic theory as practiced by Noam Chomsky and his followers.</td><td>This much detail is optional.</td></tr>
<tr><td>The Hidden Life of Language also discusses Chomsky's theory, but in a more general way, as part of one chapter. It presents a much wider selection of topics than Pinker's</td><td>Similar but different; implies hers as more meaningful to public.</td></tr>
<tr><td>book. At around 200 pages instead of 494, it is also less daunting for the average reader.</td><td>Contrasts length to support greater accessibility for her lay reader.</td></tr>
</table>

- Use shortcuts to reduce reading; and
- Write your "About the Competition."

CHECK RECENT OUT-OF-PRINT TITLES

Publishers today tend to let books slide into demise at a faster rate than in the past. Although small to mid-sized publishers make every effort to keep a book active in what is referred to as their "backlist," larger publishers may not keep your first printing in stock or maintain reprints, even with apparently acceptable sales. For one thing, publishers must pay a tax on books they warehouse from one tax year to the next, so they have little incentive to keep slower-moving inventory.

Cumulative Books in Print will help you catch other titles that meet the five-year-or-less criteria.

USE SHORTCUTS TO REDUCE READING

Through your research, you've collected the list of titles and some library descriptions for use in the competition section. You may have one or one hundred. Since you will have to provide a paragraph or two of description and analysis about each truly comparable book, you would not want to spend months or years reading through *every* title you've researched. There are ways to trim this task to a manageable size.

Assuming you have already eliminated dissimilar titles, ask a reference librarian to help you locate book reviews of the other books remaining on your list. Reviewers usually provide enough description and analysis for you to fairly compare your idea with the published book. If your book is similar, then determine if the review provides enough material to draft the one or two paragraphs you'll need.

For books on your list for which no adequate reviews exist, you must locate them at your library, through interlibrary loan, or in bookstores. If you still have dozens of books that qualify, gathering a stack may sound like a year's work, but don't panic; you're not going to "read" them all. Your job is to extract the details you need by reading the book jackets, scanning the indices, studying the tables of contents, and spot-reading enough to confirm or deny your conclusions.

The book jacket summarizes a book's essence. From the contents and index you can determine how a book differs from yours. In a well-written book, you can read the introduction, chapter one, and the last few pages of the book to glean a succinct summary of an author's purpose or a book's theme, as well as its slant—exactly what you need for your description and analyses.

By the time you apply this scanning method to the books you intend to describe, you'll only have a few books left—those books most like your own. *Read them.* Take notes about their similarities to and differences from yours. And, read them to learn how other authors handle the job of writing a book on your subject.

Write Your "About the Competition"

With your research notes and bibliographic information on each title you plan to include in your competition section, you're ready to write. This section of the proposal should contain the following parts:

- Lead;
- Analysis of each book, including:
  - a listing of bibliographic data about each competitive title;
  - a description of each book;
  - a comparison and contrast of each book with yours; and
  - transition paragraphs; and
- Conclusion.

LEAD

In the lead or introductory paragraph, you should restate the subject—and possibly the background—of your book to indicate why it should be published now. Redefine your targeted reader and generate excitement. You

> Remember, as in all sections of your proposal, plan to sell what is different and special about your book, emphasizing your authority to write it.

may add a reminder of your credentials. In other words, constantly sell your book and yourself.

Take another look at Rosemarie Ostler's lead in Sidebar 4-1. Compare her style and sales approach to instructor Val Dumond's lead paragraph below from the competition section for her book *Grammar for Grownups*:

I am always looking for useful books about grammar to recommend to students, business clients, writers of all kinds. Whenever a new class is scheduled, I dash hopefully to the bookstore to pick up the latest and best grammar guidelines only to discover that while there are many grammar books out there, none wants to help grownups apply the rules they already know in an organized easy-to-understand approach.

In this one short lead, the author has reminded us of her audience—students, business clients, and writers. She's reminded us of her qualifications—she teaches grammar; and she's put us on notice that none of the existing books satisfy the needs of her students. She's done something else: she's given us a sample of her warm personal style, which we must believe will be the style of her book as well.

Biochemist Linda Jean Shepherd, Ph.D., uses her lead for the competition section of her book to reiterate the benefits her book offers to readers, and to keep generating excitement.

> *Lifting the Veil: The Feminine Face of Science* is a book that integrates the exciting trends of the new sciences and the related, holistic world view that is a gift of the feminine. It uses the actual experiences of scientists to help readers reconnect with the enlivening qualities of themselves and counteract the arid, one-sided masculine approach to the world.

ANALYSIS OF EACH BOOK

Limit your analysis of each competitive book to no more than three short paragraphs. If you have several categories of books—perhaps matching different targeted markets—provide headings for these markets.

List Bibliographic Data

Introduce each title by listing bibliographic data, including author, title, publisher, publication date, and, if possible, retail prices, hardback or paperback, and edition. There are two basic styles to do this. If you lean toward a well-ordered universe, you might prefer a more organized presentation, first listing the bibliographic data and then describing and analyzing each book. If you're the type who leans toward the artistic side, you might prefer to present the same data but in a more casual style that works the information into the paragraphs. (I've been told that these two styles correspond to left-brain or right-brain dominance, as well as to IBM owners versus Macintosh owners, but I don't believe it!)

I prefer a more organized style for graphic clarity and, therefore, clarity of content. The five coauthors of *Mothering Twins* demonstrate this more formal style:

> *Twins From Conception to Five Years* by Averil Clegg and Ann Woolett (from Great Britain), Van Nostrand Reinhold Co., revised edition, 1988. (127 pp.), $11.50.
>
> A short, practical guide written in an outline format with suggestions often listed for the reader. It supports women in making individual choices concerning pregnancy, birth, and early care of twins... It does not address the emotional side of having twins.

In her proposal for *Five Days to an Organized Life*, time management consultant Lucia H. Hedrick uses a more open, narrative style. Here is an one of her descriptions of the competition with the bibliographic data worked into the paragraph:

> In the books-for-homemakers category, Stephanie Winston's *Getting Organized* (Warner, 1978) and Pam Young and Peggy Jones' *Sidetracked Home Executive* (Warner, 1982) stand out among other offerings, especially for their sense of humor, but I quarrel with Young and Jones' preoccupation with keeping life in a file box and their insistence on written reminders for tasks which are automatic. I wonder if I would forget to flush unless I had written it on a file card!
>
> Winston's book is concerned very much with organizing things rather than time. In contrast to both *Five Days* is devoted to showing *how to achieve self-satisfaction by spending time doing what you want to do.*

As you can see, the description and analysis of a competitor can take up only one or two paragraphs, and it is far from a complete summary of the book's contents.

A Description of Each Book

Don't aim to be neutral; as a proposal writer, your job is to show your book in a more favorable light than those you list.

Notice how the author of *Five*

> Select the most important highlights that demonstrate the similarities and differences you wish to emphasize.

Days to an Organized Life left no doubt about the contrasting (plus different and better) feature of her book by underlining that feature.

Let's consider one more example. The following presents one of two books listed in Dr. Derek S. Lipman's book on stopping snoring:

> *Snoring*, by Marcus H. Boulware (American Faculty Press, 1972), was written by a speech therapist. Because its publication preceded the establishment of sleep disorder laboratories and the development of the surgical procedure known as UPPP, this book no longer provides current medical information on the subject.

Thus, Dr. Lipman made short order of a competitive title in a field where he found only two books on his subject.

Comparison and Contrast of Each Book With Yours

Notice, too, that all three authors show respect for other authors, yet emphasize their book's shortcomings. Criticize your competitors but don't insult them. Realize that your proposal might end up in the hands of an editor who acquired and loved one of the books you feel inclined to trash. For my taste, I thought Lucia H. Hedrick should have deleted her one line, "I wonder if I would forget to flush unless I had written it on a file card!"

When your book is similar in content, style, or theme, use phrases such as: "similar to, in a like manner, also, the same as." When highlighting your book's superiority and differences, use transitional phrases, such as: "in contrast to, unlike, different from," and use superlatives, such as: "much wider, less daunting, stronger sense, more defined, broader, more inclusive."

Transition Paragraphs

Paragraphs before or after particular profiles help interpret your conclusions and orient an editor to view the competition the way you would like. Use of "sandwich" paragraphs also works most effectively to make a transition from the competition profiles in one market, such as "self help," to another, such as "women's psychology."

Transition paragraphs are also a necessity to explain why you would profile books not directly related to your subject. Perhaps you don't find any directly similar books. But, you do find others that are similar in style, format, or theme, although not in subject. Perhaps a book mentions your subject, but only in one chapter. Or, you may decide to describe novels in order to show the popularity of your nonfiction subject. Use transition paragraphs for explanations prior to offering your profiles and analyses.

CONCLUSION

Conclude your "About the Competition" section by summarizing the superiority of your book. Continue to sell excitement. For example, consider linguistics educator Rosemarie Ostler's conclusion:

> In short, the three books described above fail to provide the reader with the same scope of information as *The Hidden Life of Language*. Either they do not mention modern theories of language or they focus heavily on cognitive-neurolinguistic aspects. In contrast, this book presents detailed yet nontechnical analysis of casual and regional speech, a summary of the latest findings on language origins, and substantive but easily-grasped details of language change, as well as current information on the neurological and psychological aspects of language. This breadth of outlook cannot be found among the books now available.

Troubleshooting

Use the following list to diagnose problems in writing "About the Competition." Then apply a remedy from the suggestions that follow.

- The where-to-shelve dilemma;
- Too few comparable books; or
- Too many comparable books.

THE WHERE-TO-SHELVE DILEMMA

Perhaps, your dream is to walk into your local bookstore and see 100 copies of your book on a publisher's stand next to the cash register, not in the bowels of the store. Dream on, but in your proposal, get real.

What's the big deal? The big deal has to do with distribution, delivering the goods to your customers. If a book doesn't fit a clear shelving category, then it risks being put somewhere your reader may not think to look. If your book's success doesn't depend heavily on bookstore sales, then the impact of shelving is, of course, lessened.

The successful sale of a book may depend on whether a bookstore owner can place it on the right shelf to reach the customer who habitually browses in only one area of the store.

What can you do? To some degree, sharpening your title may be the answer. In chapter two, we discussed the advantage of a descriptive, but perhaps boring, title over a cute, but obscure one. Everyone in publishing—including booksellers—complain of overload. Even John Baker, Editorial Director of *Publishers Weekly* complained that too many books and too many different books are being published. If the shelving location (and therefore, possibly, the market) for your book is not clear from your title, make doubly sure it is self-evident from your subtitle. Otherwise, an overloaded bookseller may mis-shelve it and your customer miss it.

Consider psychotherapist John Gray's bestseller, *Men Are From Mars, Women Are From Venus*. Science fiction? Astronomy? Religion? Okay, probably everyone gets the implied joke and guesses this is a book about relationships and the struggle between men and women. But Dr. Gray has made sure we do. Check out his subtitle: "A Practical Guide for Improving Communication and Getting What You Want in Your Relationships." He leaves no room for doubt. The where-to-shelve dilemma is resolved.

Certainty about shelving means a clear, definable market. If you decide that your book fits more than one shelf in a bookstore, then your headings in "About the Competition" should reflect these different markets. Diagnostically, if you come up with more than one shelf for your book, you could be writing for too broad a market. Ask yourself, "Can I narrow my book to one readership?" If you can't, if your book reaches more than one category of reader because it is cross-disciplinary, then you may have a crossover problem.

Books with multiple readerships are called "crossover" books, because they ask readers to cross over from their favorite subject areas and peruse unfamiliar shelves and subjects. Some books have no clear single shelf because they include many disciplines of study and may confuse the retailer and, then, fall through the cracks. Beyond the where-to-shelve dilemma, you may have too many audiences with no single audience strong enough to carry your book.

Recall from the start of this chapter my question about psychologist Marilyn Barrett's proposed book. She divided her competition section into three categories: nature and ecology, gardening, and self-help. She introduces her section with a lead that explains why she made these choices:

Creating Eden: The Garden as a Healing Space is a book that integrates exciting trends in gardening, holistic environmentalism, and self-help psychology. It uses the actual *and* metaphoric garden to help readers reconnect with the restorative processes of nature, feel more balanced and aware of themselves and counteract the treadmill effect of urban living.

Dr. Barrett's decisions about where her book would be shelved seem well-thought-out and accurate, but let's look into this further.

Do you sense a compatibility between her three categories—nature/ecology, gardening, and self-help? On the surface, my answer is yes. On closer examination, I'm not sure. Many ardent gardeners haven't expanded their interests or philosophies to nature and the environment. Certainly neither environmentalists nor gardeners are necessarily self-help readers. I believe Dr. Barrett's most dominant market is self-help, but a specialized nature-loving, garden-loving, self-help reader. Fortunately, they number plenty.

If you, too, have defined more than one market in your competition, make sure that the divergent categories are few, perhaps two or three, and that each category has a solid reading market. For instance, I recently purchased *The Long Quiet Highway* by Natalie Goldberg. In fact, I was surprised to find it where I was browsing—autobiographies—because I associate her with a book for writers called *Writing Down the Bones*. In a moderately sized bookstore, you'd find copies in both locations, even though *The Long Quiet Highway* is an autobiography more than a book on writing. That's because booksellers want to capitalize on name recognition and capture her prior readers. Yet, the fact that I found her book in autobiography tells me that the retailer read the jacket and also hoped to pick up readers whose allegiance runs to autobiography. In any case, she has a solid market for both shelves.

Consider *Mysteries of the Dark Moon*, a book about seeing and using the difficult, i.e. "dark," experiences of life, written by self-described mythologist and counselor Demetra George. She lists her comparable or competitive books under two categories: (1) women's psychology and (2) new age, personal growth/healing, and recovery. Separating the catchall of the latter category could produce a total of four possible shelving choices, not two.

With this expanded number of categories, Demetra George hoped to demonstrate a wide market and draw the interest of a larger publisher.

Mysteries of the Dark Moon: The Healing Power of the Dark Goddess was published by Harper San Francisco (a division of HarperCollins). Obviously, Harper editors saw the potential for the book and must have believed the many markets were compatible, rather than producing a crossover problem. It's also possible that Demetra George had demonstrated a following, name recognition, and loyalty from readers of her two prior books, which had been on astrology. While the combination of book idea, description in "About the Market," and author credentials worked for Demetra George, you should know that multiple markets always mean some risk of being perceived as a crossover problem.

If your book seems to cross subject lines, go back to the drawing board and ask yourself if you should alter your idea. Perhaps it needs further simplifying and narrowing. Reread chapter two on refining ideas. You may have thought you had a well-defined slant, but perhaps you need to change your slant to identify a more definable audience. At the very least, visit a well-stocked bookstore and ask the manager to help you determine your primary market and define the categories that you can use in "About the Competition."

TOO FEW COMPARABLE BOOKS

When Dr. Darold A. Treffert proposed his book on savants (gifted but mentally impaired individuals), he had no comparable books to put in his competition section. He could have risked editorial rejection based on, "It's never been done," except for one fact. Several other sections of his proposal made mention of his own recent appearances on *CBS Evening News, That's Incredible, Donahue, 60 Minutes,* and other shows. His credentials as a specialist on the savant

> Remember that less is more, especially in writing. Rethinking your book at this point might be the best thing you ever did.

syndrome inspire awe, and he'd already taken steps to put the fascinating subject before the public. His book was published under the title *Extraordinary People.*

If you find no other popular books on your subject, it could mean your idea is too obscure for mainstream publishing.

If you have academic or professional qualifications, you may need to pitch your book to a university or technical publisher. Or, ask yourself whether you've included too much for one book, or only enough for a long magazine article. If you decide that your idea is worthy of pursuit *as is*, then be willing to go to extra lengths to win over a publisher. You may need to postpone marketing until you expand your credentials. On the other hand, the problem may be remedied by nailing down more statistics that prove your book will have a large market. Emphasize the section promising your willingness to promote the book.

Another strategy for putting "something" in this section is to mention and describe recent articles in popular magazines or even novels, in order to build a case for the public's growing interest. Lay historian and travel writer Susan Lloyd worked hard to overcome the paucity of books related to her latest project, *The Last*

> If you find few or no books like yours, stop all work on your proposal until you determine why.

Zapatista: Beginning with her introductory paragraph printed below, she builds the case for why a book on a Mexican folk hero is worthy of publication.

> Because of his popularity and timeliness of subject, *The Last Zapatista* represents the kind of book, touching on history, myth, politics and travel, which is of interest to the general reading audience. Never has the subject of Mexico, in particular, been of such interest to the U. S. public because of a recently passed trade agreement, rebellion brewing in Mexico's south, and an ever-growing Mexican population north of the border. Attesting to its popularity, it is interesting to note the number of books on Mexican or Latin American subjects that have been made into feature-length Hollywood films—including many books in this competition listing. It is also exciting and especially timely that a feature Hollywood film is being made about Zapata, scheduled for release in 1995.

Having surrounded her book with popular interest from political events in Mexico and from novels and movies, Susan Lloyd then supports these claims with several paragraphs that position her book with Latino classics and bestselling Mexico-based novels, including: *One Hundred Years of Solitude* (Marquez), *The House of the Spirits* (Allende), *Like Water for Chocolate* (Esquivel), and *The Mambo Kings Play Songs of Love* (Hijuelos).

In the subsequent paragraphs of her competition section, she introduces novels where Zapata is mentioned or featured. She cites a planned

Hollywood movie for one. For others, she ties their settings to the current *zapatista* uprising in Chiapas—a reminder to editors about her book's timeliness.

Occasionally, a book is rejected, not because it wouldn't be great, but because it is literally ahead of its time, the first in a new field. Before you decide you might just be the next Rachel Carson (ecology), Paul Erlich (environmental philosophy), Marilyn Ferguson (new age), Stephen Hawking (science), or Paul Senge (business), do some deep soul-searching. Most of the time, writers of "firsts" find no comparable books because their subject is:

- too specialized or obscure;
- too limited to produce a large enough readership to warrant book-length treatment; or
- too broad. Instead of being a book written for everyone, it becomes a book written for no one.

Nevertheless, if you genuinely believe you have something new to share with the world, establish credibility by writing and publishing magazine articles on your subject, give workshops, gather endorsements from recognized authorities in the field—before seeking book publication. Doing so is a great test of your ideas and should make even clearer whether yours is a pearl of great price or a good-looking but valueless imitation.

If your book is at the cutting edge you may need to market directly to a small or specialty publisher of books in your field, rather than seeking an agent for sale to a larger publisher and a general-interest reader. Success with a small publisher may lead to word-of-mouth sales and ultimately to a reprint by a larger publisher.

TOO MANY COMPARABLE BOOKS

I'll never forget the elation of my son when in second grade he "discovered" knock-knock jokes. He couldn't wait to try them out on me and was stunned when I knew the punch lines. "You've heard it before?" he asked, eyes wide with surprise.

When your search in Bowker's *Books in Print* exhumes dozens, or perhaps hundreds, of titles apparently similar to yours, you may experience a shock similar to my son's. Your book may have already been done.

Your contribution must be a substantial enough addition to warrant book-length treatment.

Business consultant Lucia H. Hedrick faced and overcame this problem for her book, *Five Days to an Organized Life*. Can you imagine

> Read deeply enough on your subject to assure yourself, agents, and editors that you have something to add to the field.

her task, having to first convince her agent, Denise Marcil, and then editors, that we really do need another book on getting organized? Literally, hundreds have been published on the subject. In fact, knowing that any sane agent or editor would think of this immediately, the second sentence in her proposal reads, "There are more than 300 organizers, or personal planning aids, on the market...[with sales] expected to exceed $300 million."

With the flooded field acknowledged up front, she goes on to convince the proposal reader why hers *is* different *and* better. In her "About the Competition," she escapes the task of itemizing hundreds of these competitors with a first sweeping contrast:

> ...There are many books available on personal organization, including a few "classics," but they are too long. Like so many self-help books today, they are ninety percent filler and ten percent substance, the kind that cause my students to throw up their hands and cry, "But I don't have time to read it!" After reading *Five Days*, no one will ask, "Where's the beef?"

Later she practices the organization she preaches by stating:

> In a sea of many titles, organization books fall into four categories, based on target audiences: those written for executives, for homemakers, for women, and the general organization guides.

Having established this distinction, she then introduces representative books for each category, only two or three, as if these few competitors represent the same strengths and failings of all of the rest of the books in that category.

This author cleverly elevates her book above all others in this crowded field by this summary paragraph:

> In short, *Five Days* is a nuts and bolts—knit one, purl two— kind of book. Its approach is different from previous works in three ways: 1) *brevity*: it makes its points in fewer pages, 2) *philosophy*: I emphasize rewards and having fun, and 3) *mechanics*: I keep it

simple...

Her argument in favor of her system so convinced me of its worth that I felt an urgency to read her book. I quickly found that it had sold out in all the bookstores in my city. She transferred her conviction and enthusiasm so effectively that I waited impatiently for the book to come in. I wouldn't even look at a competitor's system. That's a successful "About the Competition!" With over 80,000 books sold to date, the author has also transferred that enthusiasm into the book.

About the Author: Selling Yourself

Chapter Goal: To present yourself and your qualifications in the best possible light.

Years ago, I hammered out resumes for people as part of a business. I suggested that my clients write down their job histories and make notes about other accomplishments, such as awards, memberships, and volunteer activity. Most of the time, independent of education or job status, my clients arrived at my office with a meager and incomplete record. Some brought old resumes, but most people "forgot" relevant accomplishments. Don't make that mistake in your proposal. Parade your accomplishments, your experience, and your virtues. Sell yourself to help sell your book idea.

Definition and Purpose

"About the Author" is the section of your proposal where you must detail your qualifications to write the book you propose. While this section may seem like a resume, it varies in format and style. Its purpose is to impress agents and editors and make a publisher trust you with a five-figure capital investment in your idea.

Vocation, personal experience, research, or hobby/recreation encompass the most common ways to show qualifications to write a book. Less common ways include: celebrity status—Nancy Reagan's astrologer or Prince Charles' valet—or access as a coauthor or writer-for-hire to a celebrity or expert. Nowadays, larger publishers give considerable weight to an author's connections—how many people you know in your field or in media who can aid in your book's promotion. As literary agents Mary Alice Kier and Anna Cottle put it, "...more and more New York houses actually look for a national franchise on the aspect of [author] credentials."

Sidebar 5-1

Sample: About the Author

Dean Walker is a Licensed Professional Counselor and a Child Development Specialist in Eugene, Oregon. Dean is a member of both the mental health and school counseling divisions of the Oregon Counseling Association. He has a Master of Sciences in counseling psychology and 15 years of experience in the field of human relating.

In those 15 years, Walker has worked with a variety of children ranging from incarcerated juvenile delinquents, the developmentally disabled, to "talented and gifted" children. As a child and family therapist for four years at The Child Center, a treatment facility for emotionally disturbed children in Springfield, Oregon, he developed an astute professional understanding of the deficits that plague the relationships between parents and children in dysfunctional families.

As a Child Development Specialist for the past 5 years, Walker has made school a psychologically safer, saner experience for hundreds of boys and girls at Laurel Elementary School. He also has created a parent education program that has gained wide participation from parents. Attendance at his parenting seminars total over one thousand. This year, he is participating in a groundbreaking, federally funded program that trains teachers and parents to relate as a unit in order to further the education and mental health of children.

Articles on parenting by Walker published in local newspapers and magazines have drawn invitations to speak to groups of parents in Oregon communities. He has also been published in national parenting magazines, such as *Sesame Street Magazine Parents' Guide* and *Parenting*.

Because "About the Author" requires no research, you should craft a rough draft after you've written "About the Competition." Writing this section early can give you an objective reflection of your authority to write the book, as essential as the merits of your idea itself. A rough draft of this section should make you feel certain you possess the qualifications to write the book, or signal you to suspend work on your proposal until you've developed the necessary credentials. If you remain in a quandary, see the later section of this chapter called "Troubleshooting."

Last of all, this section of the proposal should give an agent/editor a sense of who you are as a person, not just as an authority, without going into excessive personal detail.

Style of Writing

Because this is an easier section of the proposal, its guidelines are simple. Write in first- or third-person, though most writers use third-person. Speaking about yourself from this narrator's position lets you tout your qualifications without sounding like an egomaniac. First-person, however, may be perfect for a book of a highly personal nature. The advantage is that you can express your qualifications in a personal way.

This section resembles a résumé, but your qualifications should be expressed in complete sentences and paragraphs, not in lists or fragments. If the number of credentials calls for it, include a résumé in your proposal appendix.

Present your author qualifications with active, exciting verbs, rather than dull to-be verbs. Aspire to using only one to-be verb per hundred words. Emphasizes specifics over generalities, i.e, "past president of the Business Association" rather than "active in trade groups." Finally, present your credentials in descending order of importance.

Before discussing what content to include in "About the Author," read the following example, partly chosen for its brevity. This "About the Author" was written by counselor and child-development specialist Dean Walker for his book titled *Organic Parenting*.

The Six Parts of "About the Author"

While this section may seem like a standard résumé, it's a different way of presenting yourself to the world. Here's a list:

- Subject credentials;
- Career credentials; .

- Educational background;
- Credits (awards, publications, and memberships);
- Promotional skills; and
- Personal data.

SUBJECT CREDENTIALS

By the time agents or editors read "About the Author," they will presumably have already read other sections of your proposal. Some agents and editors, however, will flip from "The Concept Statement" to the author section, wanting to assess the importance or competency of the author before reading any further. For this reason, you must continue to sell yourself in this section.

Although subject qualifications and career credentials often overlap, some writers seek to publish books unrelated to career. Then, subject credentials must come from other sources, such as research, hobbies, co-writing with an expert, or personal experience.

Susan Lloyd's first book, *No Pictures in My Grave: A Spiritual Journey in Sicily*, is based on personal experience. Even though she received artist's fellowships and other funding related to her book's theme and setting, and even though she produced and directed an award-winning documentary related to the book's theme, she opened her "About the Author" in a highly personal way that matches her book's introspective tone.

> My experience growing up in Oregon in an Italian-American Catholic family provided the initial nucleus of remembered experience *for No Pictures in My Grave*.

The lead paragraph provides details about the author's grandmother and how she taught the author to pray to the Madonna. A second long paragraph develops the author's personal relationship to her education and her discovery of the Black Madonna, a key metaphor in her book.

Another writer made a lifelong study of his passion, economics, but his advanced degree and life work had led him into business administration. He pursued two strategies to overcome the deficiency in his qualifications. First, he collected "Advance Scholarly Review and Endorsements" on his book from recognized professors, authors, and scholars in the field of history. After his persuasive presentation got him an agent, he and his agent placed these reviews and endorsements directly after "The Concept

Statement," *before anything else* in the proposal. Not only did these endorsements supply missing credentials, he had also captured several awards for papers in economics "way back when" in his undergraduate work. While he was not, on the surface, qualified to make a scholarly contribution to the study of economics, his subject credentials supplied everything he needed to gain an agent and then a publisher.

CAREER CREDENTIALS

Your work may offer the inspiration for your book idea. If so, put your professional qualifications first in the lead paragraph of the author

> List and develop your career credentials in descending importance.

section. The sample of this section from a proposal on parenting by Dean Walker matches his career area, counseling parenting and children. His qualifications to write on this subject are identical to his career credentials. Three out of his four paragraphs address his subject qualifications that have been developed through his career.

Another professional, Dr. Derek S. Lipman, M.D., gains his authority to write a book on stopping snoring not just because he is a medical doctor, but because he specialized in otolaryngology. (I had to look that up; it means he's an ear, nose, and throat doctor.) Dr. Lipman's second sentence in his "About the Author" states: "He has studied at leading sleep disorder centers in Europe and the United States...." Thus, he has put his most relevant career credentials first.

Another doctor, a naturopathic physician proposing her book titled, *Body Salts: The Way to Health, Naturally*, opens her author section with the short and sweet statement:

> Dr. Skye Weintraub is a graduate of the National College of Naturopathic Medicine in Portland, Oregon. She specialized in homeopathy and botanical medicine.

Her status as a naturopath gives her the qualifications to write any book on natural health, but her specialty in homeopathy and botanical medicine supports why she could write a book on the limited, if not esoteric, subject of body salts.

Writing instructor Val Dumond, author of *Grammar For Grownups* offers a unique variation in how to open with subject/career qualifications:

Val Dumond has taught courses in business writing and grammar over the past ten years to government clerks and managers, college students, business executives, secretaries, lawyers, nurses, sales representatives, loggers, utility workers, shipbuilders, law officers, data processing staffs. (A list of clients is found on the following page.) After a day-long intensive session of Grammar For Grownups, their evaluations of her techniques include comments like *fun, time went fast, forgot I knew that much, enjoyable, useful, wow! I already knew that stuff.* [her italics]

This opening to "About the Author" does a lot of work for her. Notice how she presented her career credentials—ten years teaching—but how clever to give a listing of the walks-of-life of her clients. This alone delivers the message: my experience is vast, the book's contents are based on different people's needs, and my market has a potentially large audience. Last in the paragraph, she closes with client endorsements of the most potent kind—students who have been exposed to her method. Sales!

Her career credentials continue with a mention of prior publications of grammar books. You'd think she would have opened with this publishing credit, but since her other books were published by Prentice-Hall and probably found an academic audience, she might have chosen not to plant the idea of that audience in her agent/editor's mind. In contrast, *Grammar for Grownups* is aimed at a general readership.

EDUCATIONAL BACKGROUND

Generally speaking, any degree from the masters level up carries weight, independent of the subject of your book, but agents are wary of book ideas

> Decide whether your level of education helps or hinders your success, and feature it accordingly.

written by academicians. You may be qualified, but you'll have to demonstrate an ability to translate your knowledge into the style of writing enjoyed by your particular audience.

In some cases, I instruct erudite clients to bury the mention of their doctoral theses, or sometimes their doctoral degrees *until* they've interested the reader in their subjects.

When linguistics educator Rosemarie Ostler contacted me regarding her proposal for a book titled *The Hidden Life of Language*, she had no claim to fame and no writing credits except in academic journals. A Ph.D. in Linguistics formed the sole basis of her authority for writing a book and served as her strongest credential for the author section. Thus, her lead paragraph reads, "Rosemarie Ostler received her Ph.D. in Linguistics from the University of Washington in 1984, and has taught at the university level." Incidentally, the first several drafts of her proposal and sample chapters read like (yawn) a textbook. Like psychologist Marilyn Barrett who based her book on a scholarly thesis, Rosemarie Ostler also had to rewrite several times to make the transition from thesis-speak to reader-friendly writing. Her final proposal and agent representation is proof that a Ph.D. can unlearn *academese*.

> Never mislead anyone about your qualifications. Highlight or underplay, yes; embellish, no!

Neither Val Dumond (*Grammar for Grownups*) nor Lucia H. Hedrick (*Five Days to an Organized Life*) list their educational backgrounds. Their degrees may be irrelevant, possibly because they are in areas different from their books' subjects, or unimportant against the weight of their other credentials.

Susan Lloyd made a similar choice by listing her Bachelor of Science degree in Art Education and Master of Fine Arts degree in Photography/English in the last paragraph of her author section for her inner-journey book, *No Pictures in My Grave*.

If your educational degrees or nonacademic training seem relevant to your project, make sure they appear early in the author section. Also indicate the specific college or university where you earned them. If your education is not particularly relevant, you have no pressing need to do this. However, if you have graduated from a prestigious institution, mention your degree and the institution, whether or not it is directly relevant. In other words, you're allowed the sin of omission, or the sin of inclusion, in presenting your credentials. Just know that when you leave information out, you may be subject to wild speculation, which may or may not be to your advantage.

In addition, never include a comprehensive accounting for every school you attended or every job you've held. List only items that relate to your proposed book.

CREDITS (AWARDS, PUBLICATIONS, AND MEMBERSHIPS)

Awards indicate that you rose above others to receive recognition. Publications show your success as a writer. And, memberships suggest current interest and involvement. All three count.

Awards

Awards might include grants and fellowships to pursue work, such as Susan Lloyd's Oregon Arts Commission Individual Artist Fellowship Award, her *Flying Springbok* Writing Competition Award, and her Helen Wurlitzer Foundation Writers in Residence Grant, all included in her author section and, as you can see, specifically mentioned.

Perhaps you've received some award in your work; by all means include it. The same holds true for any placement award in writing contests. Whether or not you have published your writing, a contest placement demonstrates recognition of your ability.

Publications

It seems self-evident that you would include your publishing credits; after all, you're pitching a book! However, you wouldn't necessarily want to include mention of *all* your credits.

> Omit mention of any award, publication, or membership that would diminish you or your proposed work.

Several years ago, I reviewed a proposal written by a therapist. In her "About the Author" section she cited publication of articles with a magazine called *Nails*. Referring to manicure, these publishing credits added nothing to her proposal for a book about therapy. At worst, they threatened to reduce her credibility in the eyes of some agents or editors.

Be specific about your credits. For example, in the sample by Dean Walker, he mentions by name his most impressive credits with two magazines of national circulation, *Sesame Street Magazine Parent Guide* and *Parenting*.

Whether or not a book publication bears directly on your present subject, cite it by title, publisher, and date. General descriptions make a *generally* good impression. Specifics make a powerful impression. Take grammarian Val Dumond's author section, for example. She informs the reader that her *Elements of Nonsexist Usage* was released by Prentice-Hall with a first printing of 30,000 copies. Because the topic is relevant to her proposed

Grammar for Grownups, she spends a full paragraph describing its contents. She continues with specific mention of an earlier self-published project, also on nonsexist language, and describes by title her three books about history. Last of all, regarding her publication history, Dumond tells of publishing a newsletter for the past three years called *Words and Music* (being specific again) and describes its language/grammar-related contents.

Your publishing credits may range from those that are in high-circulation magazines to projects that you have published for your own enjoyment and distribution. You increase your authority to the degree that your writings reflect the subject of your proposed book and were published by nationally circulated magazines.

Memberships

Use the same criteria for including any memberships or affiliations as for the rest of author credentials: relevancy to your proposed book.

For instance, coauthors Emily Kay and Anita Saville sought publication of a biography titled, *We'll Remember in November: Molly Yard's Gift to Women's Rights*. Since the woman they featured was a past president of the National Organization for Women (NOW), it would be a strange omission were they not to mention and enlarge upon their own activities as NOW members. Consider the first of two paragraphs:

> Both Ms. Saville and Ms. Kay are long-time activists in the women's movement. Inspired by Molly Yard's call to arms, they founded a local chapter of the National Organization for Women in 1989. Through their work with NOW, they have played key roles in organizing a number of successful projects—including a fund-raiser for survivors of battering and rape, which has raised more than $100,000, and a legal advocacy network for women in Massachusetts....

Besides relevancy to your proposed book, memberships listed in "About the Author" can alert an agent/editor to your connections. They form part of the picture of your ability to promote your book.

PROMOTIONAL SKILLS

In chapter twelve, I'll show you how to develop a complete promotional plan. In the author section, however, you have a chance to present *past* experiences that display your promotional skills. Don't panic; not everyone includes something related to promotion in "About the Author." Before you quickly dismiss this "hole" in your background, consider teaching, leading seminars, making television or radio appearances, joining speaking clubs, all of which demonstrate promotion skills. Business consultant Lucia H. Hedrick devotes two paragraphs on her promotion skills, as follows:

> I am a sought-after speaker for agencies, professional associations and business organizations, including the United Way, the PTA Council, the Junior League, the National Organization for Women, the Entrepreneurial Women's Network, the National YWCA ENCORE program, the Women's Council of Realtors, and many others.
>
> As an expert on personal organization, I appear regularly on cable television, am interviewed extensively, and am quoted in the national press.

Notice the confidence with which this author projected her promotional skills. Is she successfully selling herself? I believe so, and her specific list in the first paragraph substantiates her claim of being "a sought-after speaker" a matter of fact, not of egotism.

Likewise, mythologist Demetra George, author of two prior books, shows no hesitation in presenting her promotional skills in her "About the Author," as follows:

> Ms. George is a captivating and dynamic speaker and has presented workshops in Boston, New York, Minneapolis, San Francisco, Phoenix, Seattle, Portland, and all across Canada....

This list of major cities spanning the continent telegraphs her ability to promote a book nationally and internationally. These authors offer great models for the unhesitating way you should present your qualifications.

SEQUELS OR FUTURE BOOKS

Some books lend themselves to sequels, or you may be gestating a related book idea. Add a brief description of the work. After Lucy Hedrick sold *Five Days to an Organized Life,* she sold in rapid succession, *365 Ways to Save Time, 365 Ways to Save Time With Kids,* and *365 Ways to Save Money,* seizing upon the success of her first work and the wave of number-slant and list books popular in the early nineties.

Agents and publishers seek experts who want to write more than one book. Since only about 25% of all books earn out the advance paid the author, it makes good business sense to recoup publisher investment through subsequent books. Typically, first advances are lower than subsequent ones, so agents too stand to profit by long-term relationships with authors over many books.

PERSONAL DATA

One purpose of the author section is to convey a sense of who you are as a person to the editor. Some writers elect to omit any personal data. Still, just a sentence or two can add dimension and provide a satisfying conclusion to this section. Consider Demetra George's final paragraph, which wraps personal data together with her book's concept.

> Demetra George lives on the Oregon Coast with her two teenage children whom she co-parents with their father. Her daily contact with the Pacific Ocean attunes her to the rhythms of the tides, which are regulated by the phases of the moon. She was born during the dark phase of the moon.

A bit of personal data transforms you from a mass of qualifications and credentials into a person an agent or editor might even like to meet one day.

Troubleshooting

Fortunately, "About the Author" is one section in the proposal where not too much can go wrong. If you've made an effort to include all six parts, to give specific detail, to write in a lively narrative way with lots of active verbs, then you've met the most important criteria. Only three problems come to mind:

- Minimal qualifications;
- An excess of qualifications; and
- Qualifications of more than one author.

MINIMAL QUALIFICATIONS

If you decide that you are minimally qualified—in credentials—to write your book, you must consider the appropriateness of undertaking it. Perhaps you should team up as a coauthor with an expert in your chosen subject. Perhaps you should shift into an idea that better matches your existing qualifications.

Consider what a senior editor at a large New York house has to say about minimal qualifications:

> Minimal credentials can be difficult, because book reviewers, booksellers, and everyone else will want to know why the publisher has chosen this book to publish, and why this author is qualified (other than enthusiasm) to write a book. An exciting book idea does not necessarily translate into an exciting, or even a good, book.

I remember the sinking feeling I got when one of my students approached me with a well-thought-out continuation of the thinking of philosopher and mystic, Teilhard de Chardin. Now, that's a big undertaking. My student had spent decades in deep contemplation straightening out the bugs. She worked as a computer technician with no educational credentials beyond the bachelor's level. To convince any editor that she had the authority to write such a book, she would have had to show subject qualifications, such as the publication of articles, or membership in organizations of philosophical inquiry, or serving as a famous philosopher's apprentice.

Lacking any career or subject credentials, this woman wanted her manuscript—her life's passion—to be considered on its own merits. I wish it could be so. I have heard this plea often from writers long on passion and short on credentials. Unfortunately, it's like asking Stanford to admit you because you're smart, even though you're missing a high-school diploma.

If you are committed to writing in your chosen subject area, then plan to take all the time necessary to develop missing qualifications. This may involve returning to school, writing and publishing articles, and teaching workshops or classes. It may involve travel, so that you can increase your name recognition beyond your immediate locale. In whatever ways you build credentials, save all evidence of doing so—clips of published articles, flyers about seminars, class descriptions about teaching posts, or anything else that is visual. These will find a place in the appendix part of your eventual proposal. The last time I inquired, my student with the proposal on Teilhard de Chardin had amassed a stack of rejections, but had not yet decided to build more credentials.

Sometimes an author is not so much lacking in qualifications as in the willingness or skill to fully present them. Other writers may feel quite comfortable promoting themselves. Consider how you feel about this; then, show more or less detail, more or fewer of your selling points, to present yourself in the best light.

AN EXCESS OF QUALIFICATIONS

If you've been President of the United States, what do you think you'd put on your next job application? While presidents probably don't have job applications, you can be sure they don't fill in the details of everything they've done. All they need to do is list, "Former President of the United States."

When you have stacks of credentials for a book you are writing, eliminate lesser positions and experience related to the subject. Inexperienced writers give themselves away by mentioning every publication and award, dating back to Boy Scouts or Girl Scouts and eighth-grade penmanship. Just provide your strongest and most impressive qualifications. In effect, that is what the two doctors have done whose "About the Author" I've excerpted in this chapter.

A retired scientist consulted me several years ago about a book he wanted to write on prostate cancer. He erroneously believed he was supposed to include a listing of *every* article in every journal in his decades-long career as a scientist. Not one of these articles covered prostate cancer. I suggested that he exclude the itemization of credits, instead summarizing them with a statement like: "John Doe has written and published over 100 articles in scientific and technical journals."

Another way to handle long lists of accomplishments is to give the specifics of one to three of the most impressive and then summarize the rest. If an agent/editor sees a long paragraph with long listings of credits, he or she may go from impressed to fogged out. Direct attention to what's important and immediately relevant to your book.

QUALIFICATIONS OF MORE THAN ONE AUTHOR

When five mothers of twins decided to publish a book on raising twins, they agreed they would be equal coauthors of the book. They held business meetings and writing meetings. They worked out a collaborative contract specifying how they would distribute the labor, the book's promotion, and the monies from the book's sale. In their author section, each coauthor used three to five paragraphs to describe her qualifications. Each one highlighted subject, work, education, credits, and promotional qualifications. Taken together, Albi, Deurloo, Johnson, Catlin, and Greatwood have the authority to write *anything* related to child developing, rearing, or parenting. In a sense, because they are five coauthors, their author section could have raised the problem of over-featuring their qualifications. I bet they were aware of this, because four of the five coauthors pared their biographies down to three tight paragraphs. Still, presenting themselves took up three single-spaced pages.

You must provide agents and editors with biographical details of anyone whom you consider as a more or less equal participant in your book's creation. This might include experts and their coauthors, or artists and illustrators.

The coauthor/expert duo of psychophysiologist George H. Green and freelance writer Carolyn Cotter had no collaborative agreement for their publishing partnership, until they were accepted by literary agent Denise Marcil, who requires one for all her coauthoring clients. Because George Green is the expert and conceived the five-step model their book features, his author biography was presented first in the author section. In fact, three of the four paragraphs detail his qualifications for the book.

Coauthor Carolyn Cotter penned one short paragraph about her qualifications as follows:

> Carolyn Cotter (M.B.A., with a B.A. degree in Social Psychology) is a former business manager. She also is editor for books by her husband, Richard (Prentice Hall: *The Business Policy Game, Modern Business Decisions, Commercial Banking*).

Carolyn Cotter had no publishing credits of her own prior to writing the book for George Green. Yet, this short paragraph summarized her strongest credentials while giving full billing to her coauthor expert.

If your book has substantial art work or illustrations, you should ask the artist for biographical information. This should follow your biographical data. It doesn't matter whether or not you have hired the artist, or agreed to share the advance and royalties. In some books, illustrations or photography become as invaluable to the "statement" of the work's identity as the idea and actual writing. The professional accomplishments of your artist are not only important but may compensate for perceived weaknesses in your own qualifications.

After you write your "About the Author," ask some trusted others to read it and make suggestions. Include some readers who know you well and who understand that the purpose of this section is to sing your praises. Or, ask a writer or editor familiar with nonfiction book proposals. If my experience writing resumes for others is any measure, you're more likely to be too modest than to overstate your abilities.

After you've thoroughly defined your qualifications, you're ready to move on to define your audience.

CHAPTER SIX

The Concept Statement:
Tell Me Why I Should Buy Your Book

* **The Concept Statement**
  About the Book
  About the Author
  About the Market
  About the Competition
  Production Details
  About Promotion
  Table of Contents
  Chapter Summaries
  Sample Chapters
  The Appendix

Chapter Goal: To explain the purpose, advantage, and goals of a concept statement, and show how to "hook" an agent and publisher.

It's a busy day at B. Dalton Bookseller's. The manager of the Springfield, Anywhere, branch sees a sales representative enter the store. Like other publishing-firm reps who visit large and small bookstores throughout the country, he has one goal: to sell the books carried by his publishing house, matching titles with each retailer's special needs. The larger the house, the more titles from which the rep must select and present to the bookseller.

Although booksellers rely upon reps to help select books appropriate for their stores, they can't carry everything. Their space is limited. A sales pitch must be quick; the product matched to the store's identity.

Imagine that today the sales rep has your title among the fifty he wants to sell. In the five to ten, or perhaps fifteen, seconds he has to describe and sell the book you sweated over for two years, what will he say?

What would you say? Let's be generous. You have 150 words or less, preferably 50 words, to describe your book and get your agent, editor, review committee, sales rep, clerk, and purchaser to salivate with anticipation. Those 150 words are called "The Concept Statement."

Definition and Purpose

A concept statement is a first, short summary of your book, written in a marketing style. After the title page, "The Concept Statement" provides the first words—and therefore, the first impression—to an agent/editor. It must generate enough excitement to stimulate agents and editors to read the rest of the proposal. It must clearly and convincingly describe your book's subject and why it's different or better or both. And, it may also serve as written copy for the publisher's catalog or as a script for a sales rep's rap.

Not every proposal has a concept statement set apart from the section describing the book. However, those writers who go to the trouble to create one will be rewarded many times over, because these first words can accomplish so much. Write it well enough and it becomes the fuse that ignites editorial enthusiasm in the rest of your proposal.

After editorial acceptance, "The Concept Statement" may serve as your book's "handle" and be used for prepublication catalogs and promotion. Who knows your book better, you, or some overworked editorial assistant who may or may not take the time to thoroughly read your proposal or your book?

The Six Goals of an Ideal Concept Statement

Before you can write an effective concept statement for your book, you need an even more specific understanding of what it's intended to accomplish. An ideal concept statement will reflect all parts of the proposal an agent or editor is about to read. It's like a movie theater's trailer of coming attractions. It must accomplish the following:

- Generate excitement;
- Clearly describe the subject and scope of the book;
- Convey uniqueness and timeliness;
- Make clear your book's greatest benefit and features that deliver it;
- Mention the book's audience; and
- Reveal author credentials.

As you'll see through the examples in this chapter, not all parts will be present in every concept statement. This is a more recently delineated part of proposal writing, and many writers and authors have yet to discover its advantages and use it.

GENERATE EXCITEMENT

What in the writing of my concept statement generates excitement? Granted, excitement is a subjective experience. If an editor has been searching, for instance, for a book on proposals, or knows that a niche for one

Sidebar 6-1

Sample: The Concept Statement

Because my concept statement for this book includes all of the six goals, I've used it as the sample and provided analysis of it.

Concept Statement	Analysis
Too many qualified writers are rejected out of hand, simply because they lack	Problem/audience.
insiders' knowledge of how to write	Slant: promise.
book proposals. *Nonfiction Book Proposals Anybody Can Write* answers	Subject of book generates excitement.
the plight of these writers by	Why now?
leading them in the construction	
of a report-style proposal.	Subject of book.
Because this how-to guide shows as much	Features.
as it tells by integrating successful	Excitement through
proposals into the text, it is written	features/scope.
"writer-up" instead of "agent-down."	Uniqueness.
As the most instructional book on the	Excitement through
subject, it features simplicity, step-	features/scope.
by-step directions, and offers a template	Excitement through
for standardization of the proposal format.	unique feature.
Written by freelance editor and instructor	Author credentials.
Elizabeth Lyon, NONFICTION BOOK	
PROPOSALS ANYBODY CAN WRITE	
makes liberal use of	
examples, exercises, and checklists	Features.
to guide the inexperienced proposal	Audience.
writer from inspiration through	Excitement through
finished salable proposal.	benefit.

exists, the subject matter alone may be sufficient to create excitement. If an editor has been looking for the particular kind of book you happen to offer, average writing in a proposal may suffice to yield a contract offer.

However, in most proposals, you must back up an exciting subject with writing that enhances your book idea. When drafting your concept statement, generate excitement by using:

- Active exciting verbs;
- Upbeat tone;
- Teasing or tantalizing offers;
- Statements of promise; and
- Emotionally powerful descriptions.

CLEARLY DESCRIBE THE SUBJECT AND SCOPE OF THE BOOK

Your book's title and subtitle should help describe the subject of your book. They certainly create the first impression about the subject and scope. Descriptive, accurate titles and subtitles that match the content and uniqueness of your book are better than dramatic titles—in most cases. For example, when coauthor Carolyn Cotter submitted her proposal to me for editing, it bore the title, *Don't...Even...Try!* Try what? You'd have to consult a psychic like Jeanne Dixon to know what the authors had in mind. By the time the book hit the stands, it bore the title *Stop Being Manipulated: How to Neutralize the Bullies, Bosses, and Brutes in Your Life*. Title and subtitle now reveal the book's intended content.

Select descriptions of your book that deliver a clear picture of its scope. Some books involve diverse, interwoven subjects that appeal to more than one audience. Others feature particularly complex ideas. Still others break new ground. Teacher, psychologist, and hypnotist Dr. Michael Rousell faced all three of these challenges for his innovative book *Sudden Impact: Spontaneous Events That Shape Children's Lives*. Springing from his doctoral thesis, his concept statement nevertheless needed to simplify complex and original research while still conveying his book's depth and breadth. Here's how Dr. Rousell handled this sticky wicket in the first paragraph of his concept statement:

Clinical hypnotists generally agree that hypnosis may take place at any time or place, without a formal induction, if conditions are conducive for its presence. My research reveals that the elementary classroom is teeming with hypnotic conditions. *Sudden Impact: Spontaneous Events That Shape Children's Lives* describes how the common elementary classroom abounds with hypnotic conditions that inadvertently affect students. This book reveals how the teacher-student relationship, student characteristics, and classroom conditions virtually parallel what professionals currently know about hypnosis and spontaneous trance states.

In contrast, other book ideas may be deceptively simple. This presents the author with the job of showing unseen depth, breadth, or importance enough to warrant a book-length treatment.

Tour escort and instructor Jan G. Jett had chosen the narrow subject of tour escorting for her book *Profitable Tour Escorting: A Comprehensive Guide*. Here's her concept statement:

> *Profitable Tour Escorting: A Comprehensive Guide* is a concise, practical handbook for adventure seekers who want to transform a love of travel into a career. This guide shows how to lead domestic and international tours for top travel companies or, for independent types, how to develop and organize their own specialty tour companies.

CONVEY UNIQUENESS AND TIMELINESS

An important aspect of "The Concept Statement" is to assert the way in which your book is unique. That's why it's best to develop a slant and review the competition before setting out to write a proposal. Ask yourself how your reader will benefit, in a unique way, by purchasing yet another book on gardening, business, love relations, or history. Biochemist, Linda Jean Shepherd made clear what's unique about her book in both her title and in her concept statement:

> *Lifting the Veil: The Feminine Face of Science* is a journey of discovery of the soul of science. Using stories from practicing scientists, this book explores how the long neglected feminine viewpoint can enliven science. It creates a bridge between the masculine and feminine, and invites science to welcome the contributions of the feminine principle into this masculine realm.

At this point, you may see from these examples how some phrases accomplish more than one of the six goals. A book's subject may be what makes it unique and generates excitement. Features can create excitement; so may author credentials. The reader benefit, such as Linda Jean Shepherd's

> Multiple revisions can "boil down" your concept statement and increase its potency.

of enlivening science by creating "a bridge between the masculine and feminine" can define what is timely about a work.

Be patient. Expect to polish your concept statement from the time you write the first draft until you send it to an agent or editor. I revised mine throughout the creation of my proposal and, once again, on the same day I mailed it out.

MAKE CLEAR YOUR BOOK'S GREATEST BENEFIT, AND FEATURES THAT DELIVER THIS BENEFIT

Benefits are what your reader hopes to receive from your book. Features are the vehicles for delivering benefits. As book purchasers, we might not articulate what benefit we anticipate from a given book, yet we probably register it, or we wouldn't make the purchase.

For instance, recently I bought:

A new dictionary
- Benefits: new words, latest hyphenation decisions;
- Features: more examples, derivations, synonyms, preferred usages;

Real Magic by Wayne Dyer
- Benefits: inspiration, understanding;
- Features: personal stories, lists, instruction;

Men Are From Mars, Women Are From Venus by John Gray, Ph.D.
- Benefits: to understand male "aliens" and improve my relationships with them;
- Features: examples, case studies, lists, questions and answers.

Simply put, features include whatever structures will deliver promised benefits. My proclaimed benefit to you, the reader, is that my book "guides the inexperienced proposal writer from inspiration through finished salable proposal."

Benefits may be concrete, such as saving money, losing weight, or writing a professional proposal, or they may be abstract, such as gaining understanding, becoming inspired, or being entertained. Whether benefits are concrete or abstract, features can always be nailed down to specifics.

Because you'll also need to have a firm grip on the difference between benefits and features to write "About the Book," examine real-estate investor Mabel Armstrong's concept statement in Sidebar 6-2 and study the column identifying benefits and features until you are sure you understand the differences.

MENTION THE BOOK'S AUDIENCE

Before you write your concept statement, review your book's audience and how broad—or narrow—your market will be. Sometimes, the audience defines your book's uniqueness, such as Mabel Armstrong's "women who've

---

Sidebar 6-2
Sample: The Concept Statement

Concept Statement	Benefit or Feature Identified
The Practical Woman's Guide to *Real Estate Investment* is an introductory real-estate investments' book aimed at the entry level investor. It presents the logic and process of real-estate investing in lively,	Benefit
easy-to-understand language	Feature
with examples, anecdotes, self quizzes,	Features
forms, and work sheets to help the	Features
beginning woman investor develop	Benefit
skill and confidence to get started.	Benefit
[It] brings financial independence within the reach of most women. Using	Greatest benefit
clear and understandable terms, author	Feature
Mabel Armstrong shows that investments in real estate are not easy or mysterious.	Benefit
But they are straightforward, and can be understood and managed successfully	Benefit
by women who've never invested in anything before.	

---

never invested in anything before." The audience for the book you're reading now is specific and narrowly defined: "inexperienced proposal writers."

Authors of books for general-interest readers have a tougher time defining audience than authors who are writing books aimed at a specific, and usually smaller, readership. For instance, Green and Cotter's book, *Stop Being Manipulated*, seems potentially usable by everyone. Yet because "a book written for everyone is a book written for no one," Carolyn Cotter spent extra brain-power to define who *wouldn't* be interested in her book, and why.

REVEAL AUTHOR CREDENTIALS

One of the many questions in the minds of agents or editors when they read your concept statement is, "Does the writer have sufficient qualifications to write about this subject?" A writer can, of course, become an expert, or team up with an expert to write a book on *any* subject. Without too many words, and without creating more questions than answers, work your credentials into "The Concept Statement."

Notice how I briefly took care of author credentials in my concept statement with the phrase, "freelance editor and instructor." For her author credentials in her concept statement about her women's psychology/astrology book, *Mysteries of the Dark Moon*, Demetra George writes: "mythologist and counselor." Dr. Michael Rousell writes: teacher, psychologist, and hypnotist." Make your tag equally brief, knowing that "About the Author" permits elaboration of your qualifications.

If accomplishing these six goals in under 150 words strikes you as a task of enormous proportion, you're right—but don't fret. Take as long as you must to create a rough draft. Rewrite and refine; then lay your effort aside. Get critiques from astute friends and writers, then revise again. If you end up with 200 words you can't live without, that's fine.

Another benefit of all this hard work may be the difference between a puny advance and a respectable one. Remember the number one goal of your concept statement—and your proposal—is to generate enthusiasm in agents and editors, igniting their passion for championing another worthy book. It feels great to believe in a book and want to see it published.

Critique of Two Concept Statements

Use the six goals of an ideal book concept statement listed in the beginning of this chapter. Analyze each of the two concept statements that follow. Because you may have different likes and dislikes—like any agent or editor—your analysis may differ from mine.

Title: *The Hidden Life of Language*
Author: Rosemarie Ostler, Ph.D.

Concept Statement: *The Hidden Life of Language* is for people who want to know what the Great Vowel Shift has to do with their spelling problems; why it's easy for English speakers to learn to count in Swedish, French, Spanish and even Hindi; when the "bow-wow", "pooh-pooh", and "ding-dong" theories of language origin were popular; whether *hopefully* to mean 'I hope' is here to stay. This book, written by linguistics educator Rosemarie Ostler answers these and many other questions that ordinary people ask about language. It offers straightforward yet substantial explanations for many intriguing or puzzling features of our speech.

Among other questions answered by the book are why all infants start out with the same grammar, no matter which language they are going to speak, what anthropology can tell us about language origins, why English contains so many words from French, and how someone's pronunciation of *roof* can tell you where he or she is from. This book offers a host of fascinating facts about language while revealing the details of its inner workings.

Analysis: Of the six goals, only one is not stated or implied: what makes this book unique, or to put it another way, "why this book, why now." To add this would take only minor revision, such as a simple phrase like, "unlike any current book on language," Or, "unique by addressing the interests of the general public," or, a sentence about the glut of "new" words and meanings coming into the language. If this is the case, the reader receives a clearer understanding of the audience than provided by "ordinary people." Together these two phrases about audience would distinguish this book's general market from other books aimed at linguists or scholars.

You may have also wondered what the greatest benefit is of Rosemarie Ostler's book. I believe the benefit, which is implied, not stated, is entertainment, arousing and answering reader curiosity, delivered by the feature of "substantial explanations" and "fascinating facts." Her lead in the concept statement gives us plenty of specific examples and hooks my curiosity.

I chose this next concept statement for analysis because it represents an entirely different kind of book, the sale of which is dependent upon taking the reader with the author on a vicarious journey and succeeding in a way to make the reader feel more powerful.

Title: *Return to the Mother*
Subtitle: *A Holy Week Journey*
Author: Susan Lloyd
  Concept Statement: Journey with award-winning photographer, Susan Lloyd, to Sicily, New Mexico, the Philippines, Guatemala, and Spain to witness Easter-week rites seldom photographed, in which this western reporter becomes a participant transformed. *Return to the Mother: A Holy Week Journey* documents the survival and potency of pre-Christian, but contemporary goddess rituals. It evokes the passion and mystery of these "living myths" and powerfully draws us into a journey to reclaim our own roots and sense of *communitas*. As we join the author who is of Italian and Spanish ancestry in her "return to the Mother," we too receive the gift of renewed personal power.

Critique: In 1989, when Susan Lloyd and I first worked on her proposal, we believed our principal job was to convince agents and editors that the main benefit to readers would be a vicarious journey of personal growth and exploration through Susan's experiences. We hoped her readers would feel renewed as she did. We also knew that her book idea was complex and one of a kind.

As I look over "The Concept Statement" now, I'm again struck by Susan's originality and the multiplicity of ideas. Because the book covers a lot of ground, this might have been a concept statement that should have taken several more lines. The listing of the five locations could be simplified to read "Spain and her former colonies." In rewriting, I would also state simply, "...in which this western reporter participated," instead of "...in which this western reporter becomes a participant transformed."

Another problem with this book is revealed through its concept statement. Who would you guess to be this book's audience? Catholics? Feminist/goddess readers? Cultural anthropologists? Inner journey readers? Women of Italian or Spanish ancestry? While each of these audiences might be enthusiastic about some aspect of her book, each might also be nervous about other aspects. Although *Return to the Mother: A Holy Week Journey* was the author's first proposal, a second proposal (based on the same personal experiences) became her first book to sell: *No Pictures in My Grave: A Spiritual Journey in Sicily*. This second book may have reached a readership now ready for Susan's first book; at least, her publisher has asked to see her proposal for *Return to the Mother*.

Draft a first concept statement that includes a clear statement of your book's subject and scope, and, at the same time, scores high on the pizzazz meter. Next create a list of your book's major features and corresponding reader benefits. Rewrite your concept statement to include features and benefits, as well as uniqueness, timeliness, audience, and author qualifications. Think of writing the concept statement as though the words were modeling clay; keep molding them until you arrive at an acceptable creation. Last of all, rewrite for brevity, clarity, and smoothness.

With your book idea shaped into a word sculpture, turn your attention to examining your audience and market in greater depth in the next chapter, "About the Market."

About the Market: Defining Your Reader

Chapter Goal: To provide a detailed description of your targeted readers and your market and how to reach them.

Whether I walk into my local women's bookstore or the giant university bookstore, I am awed by the tremendous number of books on the shelves.

Who buys them all?

In 1992 Americans spent $16.5 billion on books. That's six billion more than in 1970. Canada and Mexico spent billions more. And a significant portion of books published on this continent supply foreign readers with English and translated versions. When you send your proposal off to an agent/editor, you must have a clear and specific answer to the question, "Who will read this book?"

Suppose you're an old car buff. Can you describe others with similar interests who would buy a book on restoring running boards? Or, let's say you want to write a book about the next evolutionary step of human-kind—and are qualified to write it. Who is your reader? In other words, how can you direct a publisher to your book's market?

In chapter two, I asked you to define your reader in broad strokes.

Man or woman. Lover of old cars. Self-help reader. College-educated. In terms of market, you estimated the size as small, medium, or large. Now, in "About the Market," you must nail down these two concerns—audience and market. Audience describes your targeted reader in more narrow terms, such as income, educational level, marital status, and size of family. Your audience might be middle-income, college-educated, divorced women with children, for instance. Market defines a category describing your audience, such as self-help or women's psychology.

Contents

When I teach freelance writing, I like to lead my students through a kind of Rorschach test for the magazine market. We study the covers of magazines and their ads. From these, we make guesses about a magazine's reader demographics: male or female, age, occupation, income level, education, values and beliefs, and tastes. To get you in the spirit, grab a pen and paper and write thumbnail sketches of those who would buy *Backpacking*, *Bride*, and *Country Gentleman* magazines.

Granted, you would probably need to look at the covers and ads before your guesses would be completely accurate. While the cover of a magazine, like a book, must produce a click of recognition with its reader, advertisements offer the key to reader demographics. Advertisers pay big bucks to get their pictures and copy in print. They can't afford to target their products incorrectly. You can enlighten yourself about this side of publishing by contacting any magazine's advertising department and requesting a display advertising packet. Besides rate sheets and a sample or two of the magazine, you'll get a market-research report based on surveys of the readership. This report will offer statistical answers to questions of age, gender, occupation, income, and much more.

In this section of your proposal, you should adopt the same attitude as a magazine sales manager. Consider the publisher as your potential client and your book as the product they might buy. You want the publisher to be delighted with that product, and ask for more.

Read the following sample of one "About the Market" from the proposal that sold this book!

If you can find a statistic showing the success of your competition, highlight that fact—and thereby document the potential of your market. Because a book on how to write proposals targets a special-interest audience,

Sample: About the Market

The success of Michael Larsen's book on nonfiction proposals, (over 25,000 copies sold) documents the thirst for instruction in creating these key marketing tools. With approximately 50,000 books published in the United States each year, and 85 percent of them nonfiction, publishers have an ongoing demand to fill those slots in their lists. Nonfiction has been and will continue to be the best route for a first-time author to enter publishing. If the estimated half million book manuscripts circulating at any given time are an indication, the public sees writing a book as an activity accessible to anyone with the desire, a keyboard, and money for mailings. What these writiers lacks most is marketing savvy.

The proliferation of magazines for writers during the 1980s suggests a large and growing number of writers and potential authors. Below are the titles of these magazines (reaching about 300,000 subscribers), the dates they became established, and their circulation figures (source: *1994 Writer's Market*).

Title	Date Established	Circulation
Brilliant Ideas for Publishers	1982	17,000
Byline	1981	not given
Canadian Author & Bookman	1919	3,000
Canadian Writer's Journal	1985	350
Freelance Writer's Report	1982	2,000
Housewife-Writer's Forum	1988	1,200
New Writer's Magazine	1986	5,000
Small Press	1983	5,400
The Writer	1887	not given
Writers Connection	1983	2,500
Writer's Digest	1921	225,000
Writer's Forum	1970	13,000
Writer's Guidelines	1988	1,000
Writer's Info	1985	200
Writer's Journal	1982	39,000
The Writer's Nook News	1985	5,000

The enormous increase in numbers of writing magazines since 1980, and the reported deluge of proposals and manuscripts, parallels the personal computer revolution. I believe this "trend" is far from its apex. The nearly universal use of personal computers, at least in the United States, continues to spark interest in writing and publishing. Most observers agree that computers have made the creation and revision of writing physically easier, thereby removing a giant barrier to production.

A second market for this how-to guide is small but influential and should guarantee steady backlist sales. The approximately 600 agents in the United States are in a position to recommend this book to writers they would like to represent. I believe an instructionally oriented book would be received with great relief by agents. Because of the numbers of authors with whom agents communicate, great sales potential exists through this group. Currently I work, by referral, with three agencies, Cine/Lit Representation (Mary Alice Kier and Anna Cottle), Natasha Kern, and Denise Marcil. All three have expressed appreciation for the professionalism and salability of my proposal method. Because agents are on the "front lines" of the need for proposals, I am sure marketing to them would bring steady and long-term sales.

In terms of the potential for this book, the market for *Nonfiction Book Proposals Anybody Can Write* is substantial and expanding.

I was concerned that an editor might think the market was too small. In a bulletin from Writer's Digest Book Club I discovered a statistic about one of my competitor's sales. Usually this kind of data is hard to come by; some publishers consider the number of books sold as a trade secret. I wanted to position this statistic in my lead to substantiate my belief that a healthy and growing market for this book does exist. Notice the reiteration of that idea in my concluding sentence.

Whether you approach a regional publisher like Blue Heron (this book's publisher) or a conglomerate like Simon & Schuster,

> Sell your belief that you have a solid market, one sizable enough for a publisher's profit.

the editors all look to "About the Market" to answer three questions:

- Who is the audience?
- How large is the market?
- How can the market be reached?

In the rest of this chapter, I'll answer these questions, and discuss troubleshooting and special cases.

WHO IS THE AUDIENCE?

If you've been building your proposal as you work through each of these chapters, the time you've spent researching and refining your idea and writing "About the Competition" will serve you well in defining your audience. Now, however, contemplate your average reader and answer the following questions about your audience:

- **Male or Female?** Keep in mind that as many as 70 percent of all books are purchased by women.
- **Age?** Estimate by categories, such as young adult, X-generation, yuppies, baby-boomers, seniors, or describe age by decades, such as 20-30s, 40s, 30-50, or over 55.
- **Education?** A reader's level of education has a great deal to do with reading tastes. A high-school graduate is interested in different subjects and appreciates a different style of writing than a reader with a master's degree.
- **Income?** A book on "getting by" will appeal to a different income reader than "playing the futures." Feel free to place your reader in broad income categories: low, middle, or upper, rather than by gross annual income.
- **Social Class?** Generally tied closely to income, the three major social classes—lower, middle, and upper—often divide by attitudes, prejudices, buying habits, and tastes. A person thinks differently if her major concern is making the food stamps last until the first of the month or deciding whether to spend the holidays in the Bahamas or in Paris. Each group reads and buys different books.

While these basic sociological categories will get you started, go a little further. See if you can answer what media, entertainment, and publications your reader supports. Would you expect your reader to buy a book in hardback, trade paperback, or mass-market paperback? Go to the best-stocked bookstore in your area and study books like yours. Talk with bookstore personnel. You'll find answers to your questions and gain a much better picture of your audience.

Here's how real-estate investment advisor Mabel Armstrong profiled her targeted reader in her market section for *The Practical Woman's Guide to Real Estate Investment*:

> The most likely reader of *The Practical Woman's Guide to Real Estate Investment* is the 25 to 55 year-old woman who has a couple of years of college and who is grappling with the financial issues of the day. She realizes that, even if she is married, her spouse will probably not provide her main financial support for the rest of her life....
>
> ...*The Practical Woman's Guide to Real Estate Investment* is written for the woman who recognizes her need to execute a long-range financial plan, but who is not ready to attend a foreclosure auction or build a shopping mall. She needs and wants to have the advantage of real-estate investing made clear and the intricacies of the process laid out in small, easy-to-follow steps. This profile fits the majority of my readers.

Because others can be more objective toward your idea, they may suggest an audience different from the one you had assumed.

> Ask informed friends, family, and booksellers to help you define your audience to a tee.

They may or may not be 100 percent correct, but you'd do well to listen to their ideas.

HOW LARGE IS THE MARKET?

A publisher exists for almost every well-written book idea, be it ever so narrow or specialized. But, no matter how great a book idea you have, no publisher will be interested if your market is too small to make a decent profit. You, the author, may have to adjust your expectations to match your book's true market size.

Your next job for the "About the Market" section is to find statistical support for the most optimistic view of your market's size. In the sample from my proposal of this book, notice the statistical references to the market: 25,000 books sold of another proposal book, 300,000 subscribing writers to magazines on writing, 600 agents. While I don't predict the exact size of the market, these figures help create a picture of the book's potential.

Proposal writers provide most statistical support (see the Resource Directory for references) for the size of their markets by providing:

- Magazine circulation figures from periodicals to which your reader might subscribe. *Writer's Market* or *Ulrich's International Directory* are the most common references for this information.
- Number of people who belong to certain trades, organizations, or associations. Ask a librarian; consult *American Statistical Index, Encyclopedia of Associations, Statistical Sources*, and *U. S. Census*; and glean statistics from your preliminary research.
- Trends that are supported statistically, such as a 20 percent increase in whitewater rafters over two years. Ask a librarian and use the same references indicated above.
- Statistics about the numbers of books sold annually by subject, a fact accessible from *The Bowker Annual Library* and *Book Trade Almanac*.

Some proposal writers list their statistical results in a graphically appealing way. Here's how psychotherapist Marilyn Barrett presented her data for her book, *Creating Eden: The Garden as a Healing Space*. The format is her own.

Recent trends substantiate the timeliness of a book which links healing and gardening. The following facts indicate this is an idea whose time has come:

- The Gallup Poll recently conducted for the National Gardening Association lists gardening, together with walking and swimming, as one of the top three recreational activities of Americans.
- Since 1984 three articles on the therapeutic aspects of gardening have appeared in *Organic Gardening* (which now has a circulation of over a million) and two have appeared in *Prevention*.
- The *Time Magazine* cover article of June 20, 1988 entitled, "Paradise Found," mentions that:
  - 78 percent of American households garden;
  - nursery owners say business has doubled in the past few years;
  - "recent surveys suggest that the most fervent converts (to gardening) are between 30 and 49" and that "baby boomers get much of the attention, because they ac-

count for the record $17.5 billion that was spent last year on things horticultural."

Dr. Barrett's marketing section continues with five more pieces of evidence to support the size of her book's market.

HOW CAN THE MARKET BE REACHED?

In addition to knowing the size of your market, the publisher must know how to reach it. The five major markets for books are:

> Address as many of the five typical book markets as you believe apply to your book.

- Bookstores and Book Sections;
- Specialty stores;
- Institutional sales;
- Special sales; and
- Subsidiary sales.

Bookstores and Book Sections

Bookstores come in every size, from the nationwide chains—B. Dalton Bookseller, Waldenbooks, Barnes & Noble—to independent booksellers whose stores are typically smaller. As you know, you can also purchase books from book sections of grocery stores, pharmacies, airports, and one-stop shopping stores.

In the market section of your proposal, the profile of the target audience will usually reflect sales through bookstores and book sections. For instance, linguistics educator Rosemarie Ostler starts her market section as follows:

> "*The Hidden Life of Language* belongs in the growing category of books that present important scientific findings in a form appropriate for the general public. The typical reader of this book will be a college-educated man or woman with no background in linguistics."

Since her book is aimed at the college-educated reader, it is presumed that bookstore sales are one major market.

In a similar way, freelance writer Carolyn Cotter, coauthor for *Stop Being Manipulated*, writes in the "About the Market" as follows:

This book is aimed toward both men and women, professionals, and the average person in the street.... So, besides the obvious bookstore market, books will be sold in conjunction with Dr. Green's seminars, classes, and speaking engagements....

If your book is aimed at the masses, then you and the publisher will recognize that your book will be sold through large grocery stores, retail outlets, airports, as well as through bookstores. You need not specifically mention these outlets.

The five coauthors of the book on twins handled this category of the market by setting it off as follows:

General reading or specialty stores, such as children's, women's, and birth and parenting. Booksellers' conventions, catalogs, and mail order companies.

If you believe your book targets the general public, document that belief and identify less obvious markets.

Specialty Stores

A sporting-goods store stocks books on rafting. A music store sells books on music method and artists. A giant hardware store sells books on home repair and gardening. We refer to these as specialty stores because they are in business primarily to sell something other than books.

Naturopathic physician Skye Weintraub, author of *Body Salts: The Way to Health, Naturally*, sold her books in health food stores that also carry cell salts or body salts.

Literary writer Susan Lloyd suggested that her book, *No Pictures in My Grave* "...be promoted at Italian cultural centers and museums...."

Discovering and listing specialty stores where your book can be sold is especially important for anyone whose book is not a general-interest book. If your market is narrow, you will need to find specialty markets or other outlets to give the publisher confidence that your book has a solid audience and easily reachable market.

Institutional Sales

More than one small press has secured a toehold in the publishing world because of library sales. Public libraries, university libraries, and corporate libraries must stock and update books. Like bookstores and book sections of stores, institutions are an obvious market and need not be individually mentioned. However, if you believe your book makes ideal supplementary reading for a course, then do mention that fact.

Rosemarie Ostler devotes a short paragraph to the course-adoption potential for her book, as follows:

> A secondary but possibly significant market exists among teachers of survey courses on language and related topics. Few introductory books are available that do not require some training in linguistics. *The Hidden Life of Language* fills that gap.

If you can get a professor or two to commit to using your book, mention this as well. Even though Cotter and Green wrote a mass-market book with guaranteed bookstore sales, Carolyn Cotter included a paragraph on the book's potential for course adoption:

> Some college courses will be market targets. These include courses in self-improvement, leadership, psychology, stress management, etc. Dr. Green's class at the community college in Reno, for example, will certainly be using this book as a text. In addition, at least one business faculty associate already has decided to assign it to her college classes in North Carolina as soon as it is published.

Special Sales

Sometimes, perhaps rarely, a book will make an ideal promotional gift for a business. Imagine every purchaser of a food processor finding a cookbook in the box. One came with my purchase of a Cuisinart. Giant corporations are the best bet for these bulk orders. If you can find one and guarantee their order, by all means include it in "About the Market."

Subsidiary Sales

Your agent will negotiate to retain the right to sell your book to book clubs. If not, your publisher will attempt to market to them. You can use the *Literary Market Place* to find a list of book clubs. Select ones that seem right for your book and include them in "About the Market."

Susan Lloyd defined two readerships for her book, *No Pictures in My*

Grave: "spiritual travel" readers, and women's studies. Under each category, she then listed potential book clubs. For her "spiritual travel" readers, she listed book clubs as follows:

Book Clubs
> Aquarian Agent Book Club, Greenwich, Connecticut
> Intercultural Book Club, Vershire, Vermont
> Preferred Choice Bookplan, New York
> Word Book Club, Des Moines, Iowa
> Reader's Subscription Book Club, New York

In her "About the Market," Aline Renauld Prince expanded her book club listing for *Cheapskate Decorating* and added some compelling research:

Book Clubs
- Reflecting the upsurge in this category, Meredith's Popular Science Book Club changed its name as early as 1992 to Homeowners-Do-It-Yourself Book Club. "We offer virtually every home improvement book published," says Mary Freeman in *Publishers Weekly*, page 34, June 22, 1992.
- McGraw Hill's How-To Book Club (over 40,000 members) manager stated, "Home improvement is the second largest single category for us after woodworking....

After listing several more book clubs, Aline Renauld Prince points out how the eighteen projects covered in her book lend themselves to separate videos. Then she continues her marketing section listing the subsidiary sales potential of "Audio/Video/TV Trends," as follows:

- Taunton Press produces video tapes to supplement individual titles.
- Sunset Western Gardening Book is offering a CD-ROM, and updating six home improvement packages into a "New Basics" series....
- Dean Johnson of Hometime Video publishes and distributes video tapes.
- PBS television shows weekend programs geared to the do-it-yourselfer covering projects both large and small, from remodeling "This Old House," to "Sewing with Nancy."

If you foresee strong possibilities of other subsidiary sales, by all means mention them, if possible, backing them up with specific facts and figures. Other subsidiary sales include: foreign-language translations, movies, software, audio and video, and merchandise (T-shirts, dolls in your likeness, and so forth). Of all these, the multimedia market is the most volatile, least understood, and undergoing the greatest growth. You may want to talk to software experts to explore whether your book lends itself to electronic media.

Style of Writing

Make your data easy to read. Because you're likely to have listings, statistics, or other categories, make liberal use of lists, indentations, bullets, bolds, and underlines. Be upbeat and enthusiastic. The proposal is a technical report, but it is also a sales brochure designed to get your product into print.

Troubleshooting and Special Cases

Most of the difficulties that writers encounter in "About the Market" are symptomatic of problems with their concepts, rather than in presentation of market data. Two common problems and one special case are:

- Audience too diverse;
- Market extra small; and
- Market extra large, i.e. mass market.

AUDIENCE TOO DIVERSE

When you define more than one audience for your book, such as teachers and parents, or patients with a certain illness and healthcare providers, or writers and agents, you must address each market under separate headings in "About the Market." Each audience needs statistical support describing its potential size as a market, and each audience requires suggestions about how to reach it.

Having multiple audiences only becomes a problem when they are too diverse. This creates what is referred to as a "crossover problem" (discussed in chapter four). This means that one set of readers won't "cross over" subject lines to read books shelved elsewhere. This is most problematic when the material in the book aimed at one reader antagonizes or alienates the other targeted reader.

I've consulted with writers who wished to write books for both teachers and parents. Their book ideas might, in fact, serve both audiences. However, teachers are learning experts who may read material for its instructional potential. Parents often require more explanation than needed by teachers and may feel too much pressure from extensive lists of exercises and materials requirements. Teachers and parents often form entirely different readerships and require material presented differently. Same idea; two books.

I'm a crossover reader, meaning I'm one of those less-common readers who enjoys books that blend disciplines and divergent ideas. If you have thought your book would be read by many different types of readers, determine which of them would be your strongest market. Then, figure out whether your secondary audiences would be turned off for the very reasons that would attract your other readers.

For any book with a diverse readership, put on the hat of one group and look at your proposal from that point of view alone. Would you buy this book? Does it really speak to you? Can an editor count on all of your readers?

If you emerge from these questions with doubts, consider recasting your proposal for *one* of the many markets, or relegating the others to secondary, more minor status.

MARKET EXTRA SMALL

A small, dedicated readership is not in itself a problem. I remember a woman who consulted me for her proposal on a book about scuba-diving locations off the Pacific coast. She'd done impressive market research by finding out exactly how many (and where) retail stores existed in the western coastal states that sold scuba-diving gear. She'd targeted these for special sales. She had researched the numbers of divers and the growth of interest in this sport. She was ready to convince a publisher that her book would fit a niche and sell well.

She'd also researched appropriate publishers. If she had possessed fantasies of trying to sell her book to Simon & Schuster or seeking an agent to sell to the larger publishers, she would have faced disappointing rejections. Her market research defined her book as ideal for a regional or specialty publisher. For this she would not need an agent and would waste time trying to interest agents or large publishers.

While you should seek and substantiate the most optimistic viewpoint of your book's potential sales, you must be realistic. This process of estimating the size of your market and choosing the appropriate publisher is difficult for some book ideas.

The research for your proposal's "About the Competition" should have alerted you to the type and size of publishers of similar books. If your competitors' books weren't picked up by the New York publishing giants, why should yours? A small targeted audience may lead you to more realistic expectations and the pursuit of a small publisher.

MARKET EXTRA LARGE

If you have written a book with a general audience in mind, you may be unnecessarily nervous about what to put in "About the Market." How many ways can you say, "Just about everyone could benefit from my book?" Earlier in this chapter, I gave examples of how other authors wrote paragraphs defining their books as intended for a general reader or general audience. However, rarely does this one paragraph end "About the Market." More often, writers take the opportunity to continue selling their concept or their credentials by embellishing the book's qualities and its general appeal.

Consider the following description by space engineer Ralph Nansen in the market section of his proposal for *The Fourth Era: Energy from Space*, a book he believes has a general readership. His first three paragraphs reiterate the problem his book addresses and introduce his ideas as their solution.

> ...The message of *The Fourth Era* strikes a responsive chord in people. When the author talks about how solar power from space can solve the problems that seem unsolvable, the excited response from every audience is, "Why don't we get on with it?" or "What can I do to help?" Nansen's book will be read by: Policy setters in Washington; anyone and everyone connected with the oil, gas, electrical, and other energy-related businesses; environmentalists and members of the many organizations supporting them; leaders of industries dependent on affordable energy sources; technological experts; trend watchers; economists; and every sort of concerned citizen including students, professionals, executives, government employees, and anyone interested in the future of energy sources for this country and the world.

Much of this is sophisticated "schmoozing," and it is up to you whether you feel comfortable chatting. However, it's customary to add a few paragraphs to fill out the minimal information that yours is a book written for the masses and, like Ralph Nansen, to take advantage of the opportunity to drive home information about who will read your book and why.

At this point in crafting your proposal, you've answered the fundamental concerns that determine whether you should continue with the development of the rest of the proposal and book. "About the Competition" provided proof that your book supplies a demand and offers a contribution. "About the Author" validated that you have sufficient qualifications to be writing the book you envision. "The Concept Statement" helped you translate your ideas into a "mission statement." This chapter clarified the existence and size of your audience. In the next chapter, you'll learn how to integrate all of these into the all-important presentation "About the Book."

About the Book: Inform, Dazzle, Persuade

Chapter Goal: To learn how to hook and sustain agent/editor interest while introducing the subject of your book and featuring its timeliness and originality.

Throughout school, I played flute in bands and orchestras. One night in eighth grade, I got to play the much-coveted piccolo part in *The Star Spangled Banner*. I pretended confidence I didn't feel and played my best ever. I knew why. I'd practiced the solo every day for weeks. I had learned that to play well, I needed consistent practice. Thirty years later, I can still play it.

"About the Book" is your performance, your first solo. To ask you to write this section in chapter one would have been like asking you to play a solo without practice. Although agents and editors get a sample of your writing and your ideas from "The Concept Statement," "About the Book" shows whether you can deliver on the goods. If this section is poorly written, they are unlikely to read further. To write it well, however, you must have refined your idea, done research, and written the sections about the competition, author, concept statement, and market. That task probably required weeks and weeks of practice, practice necessary for a winning performance. When agents or editors read about your book, they should feel your confidence and enthusiasm, and know you are the best for the part.

Definition and Purpose

This section of the proposal expands on your concept statement. It reflects the same six goals and more. In "About the Book," you lay out your book's subject and answer agent/editor questions, such as, "Why should we publish this book?" and "Why now?" You must document your book's uniqueness and explain how the reader will benefit by reading it. You'll list special features, such as checklists, quizzes, graphs, or interviews. In addition, "About the Book" must persuade the agent/editor that your book will make a contribution to the field and fill a publishing void. Throughout the section, you generate excitement, allude to your audience, size of market, competition, and author credentials—for starters.

> If done well, "About the Book" will gain agent or editor acceptance and a request for an encore. Done poorly, it may bring down the curtain prematurely.

Because this section has multiple purposes and an organizational structure more demanding than the other sections of the proposal, I'll break everything down into steps, beginning with a sample of "About the Book" with explanatory marginal comments. The following sample is by time-management and business consultant Lucia H. Hedrick for her book, *Five Days to an Organized Life*.

Structure

By having a lead, a body, and a conclusion, "About the Book" follows the deceptively simple basic structure of all nonfiction. Because "About the Book" must satisfy many purposes, its content within this basic structure, however, is quite complex.

Imagine "About the Book" as a painting. Your book is the subject of this painting. By the end of this section, you want an agent/editor to:
- Recognize your painting's subject;
- Appreciate its importance and place in the scheme of other paintings like it;
- Feel stimulated by your use of color, perspective, and design; and
- Want others to share the experience.

Sample: About the Book

Proposal	Comments
Everyone wants to get organized. There are more than 300 organizers, or personal planning aids, on the market, and sales of organizers in 1987 are expected to exceed $300 million. Desk and office supplies manufacturers, too, are enjoying record profits: a place for everything and everything in its place.	Overview of context for this book.
Time management seminars are prominent offerings on business training menus. Likewise, get-organized articles appear in every consumer magazine with predictable regularity.	
In spite of these aids, *people are floundering.* They complain they have too much to do and not enough time. They purchase elaborate and expensive organizers, write in them judiciously for several days, but soon abandon their good intentions for more pressing deadlines.... they're spinning their wheels—they're not moving forward, and *they're not having any fun.*	Author identifies problems: floundering, no fun.
These planners are what most people think organization is all about. It's not. The real benefit of getting organized, and my personal philosophy, is *greater freedom—freedom to have fun,* to do the things we've always dreamed of doing.	Greatest benefit of book.
In our frenetic, fast-paced lives, we all have 800 things to do. Someone who has the typical view of getting organized says, "I'm only doing 600 of these things. How do I get from 600 to 800, that is, get more done in less time?"	Anecdotal quote.
I feel that's not the right approach. We have to choose the most important tasks and get rid of, or let go of, the rest. This gives us the *free time* to do what we enjoy.	Unique approach of this book.

continued

Also, getting organized is not about what most people think they need—a crack of the whip, a kick in the pants, or a mega-dose of self-discipline. Personal organization is learned, and achieved, more by the carrot than the whip, that is by *rewarding ourselves for accomplishment*.

Benefit.

As a time management consultant who has taught hundreds of men and women how to get organized, once and for all, I have observed three reasons why people feel disorganized and out of control. First, they don't have a system, a simple system for getting on with their lives, in an organized way, one step at a time.

Author qualification.

The problem.

Secondly, they need someone to show them how to use the system. *We're not "born" organized or disorganized*. Some people learn as children to put similar items together—laundry in the laundry basket, pencils in the pencil box, books on the bookshelf. Some learn to plan ahead.... And some of us are taught certain values like being on time.

More context.

Specific examples.

However, *we can be taught*, at any time, to be more organized, just as we can learn to play an instrument, to operate a computer, or to make a tasty omelet. All too often those already trained dismiss the uneducated as untrainable.

Everyday examples.

The third reason so many men and women today are overwhelmed and disorganized is because they don't *reward themselves for accomplishments*. When we give ourselves a reward—a coffee break, a walk in the park, a browse in a bookstore— after completing a job, we boost our morale as well as our energy and feel eager to tackle our next job. But...men and women have to be taught how to use rewards to increase their productivity, and self satisfaction. Furthermore, *my system emphasizes rewards*, which is unique in approaches to getting organized.

Uniqueness.

Five Days to an Organized Life, marketed as an affordable trade paperback, will provide a

continued

simple, uncluttered method for getting
organized, getting going and getting things
done. Just as I do in my classes and workshops,
I will offer specific tools and techniques for
accomplishing goals. How to break down a
goal into bite-sized pieces and how to use lists
and calendars will be shown in detail. *Five Days*
will be organized into five chapters, one for
each "day," or step in the process, of getting
organized.

The five-day framework is a vehicle for
presenting my system a little at a time, not
a structure that the reader will continue to
follow every five days.

...However, the overriding goal of
more freedom—and thus a more satisfying life—
will remain front and center. My purpose is not
to show the reader how to get more done in less
time, but rather how to get their work done so
they can relax and have fun. And most important,
Five Days will show *we earn the freedom to have*
more fun by giving ourselves some fun along the
way....

Features.

Greatest
benefit.

By the end of this chapter, you'll know how to feature your subject,
describe the context for your book, and provide a list of reader benefits
and special features. As a literary artist, the paint on your palette is words.

THE LEAD

Every good painting has a point of visual attraction, a place where the
viewer's eye is drawn. It may be a point of light, the convergence of lines,
or a burst of contrasting color. Your lead should rivet the attention of the
overworked agent or editor who wants any excuse to reject your proposal
quickly and have one less on the desk to remind him how far behind he is.

Like a painter with dozens of colors, you can choose from many types
of leads. The most common are:

- Anecdotes;
- Impressive facts or statistics;

- Quotes;
- Startling statements;
- Narratives;
- Questions; and
- Metaphors or analogies.

Each of the following examples in Sidebar 8-2 is an actual lead to an "About the Book" section.

There are other leads as well, but these are the most common. The point is to find a lead that seems to match your book and create the most powerful hook for agent/editor attention.

THE BODY

Artists draw viewers' eyes to a point on the canvas by using perspective. We've all seen a picture with a winding road. Where the road disappears into the distant mountains, it has narrowed to a single point. The end of the road—the wide foreground or the narrowed background—determines the shape or body of "About the Book," because proposal writers also make use of something similar to perspective. Years ago, agent Natasha Kern explained the structure of "About the Book" as a funnel, larger at one end than the other. After a lead, a writer could begin this section from either the wide end or the narrow end.

The wide end corresponds to a description of the social, political, or cultural context for your book. Milieu. Climate. Often, writers spell out the problem for which their books offer solutions. After drawing the backdrop for their books, they narrow the funnel for the reader by introducing their books with their unique features and benefits.

Other writers begin at the narrow end of the funnel. Following the lead, they introduce the book. They list its unique features and promise reader benefits unlike any book prior to it. Then, later, in "About the Book," they delve into deeper reasons why their book should be published by offering a profile of "our collective problems at *this time*," and by sketching the need that this book will address. From the specific book to the general climate.

Each approach has advantages and disadvantages. More proposal writers start with the wide end of the funnel than the narrow end for one powerful reason: "About the Book" must persuade an agent/editor to read on. Establishing the wider context for a book builds a case for its need. The more

Sidebar 8-2

Leads to Begin "About the Book"

Example	Type of Lead
I was late for work. My two-year-old once again refused to be strapped into her car seat. She started screaming and kicking, and this time I screamed back. I came this close to hitting her! Having kids is tough! Each day is like another test—can I make it through without doing to my child the things my parents did that hurt me so much? (*Organic Parenting*)	Anecdote.
Everyone wants to get organized. There are more than 300 organizers, or personal planning aids, on the market, and sales of organizers in 1987 are expected to exceed $300 million. (*Five Days to an Organized Life*)	Impressive facts or statistics.
Sleep…Poets have praised it and enshrined it as the ultimate metaphor for quietude…Longfellow referred to it as "night's repose"; Shakespeare, as "nature's soft nurse." For Milton there was the "timely dew of sleep," and for Keats, the exultation: "O magic sleep! O comfortable bird/That broodest o'er the troubled sea of mind/Till it is hushed and smooth." (*Stop Your Husband From Snoring*)	Quotes.
Last year, over 1,600 world scientists and Nobel laureates gathered to issue *A Warning to Humanity*. Their statement says, in part, that "…a great change in our stewardship of the earth and the life on it is required if vast human misery is to be avoided and our global home on this planet is not to be irretrievably mutilated." Among the actions called	Startling statements.

continued

for is to reduce the use of fossil fuels and to
increase the use of solar energy...
The Fourth Era: Energy from Space)

Place has a voice: At dusk in the early summer in the pea fields, we could sometimes see the chestnut- colored, white-tailed deer, like magical beings from a special world we were only temporarily visiting. (*Tales from Coon Creek Farm*)	Narratives.
What has twenty toes, four arms, and two heads, and screams loud enough to spark even the most placid of mothers into action? No, it's not a wild love scene from an afternoon soap opera, it's TWINS! (*Mothering Twins*)	Questions.
Grammar is not for kids. We were taught the rules of grammar in a way similar to the way we were taught sex, before we had a chance to experiment. The rules, therefore, became meaningless until we had some experience for reference. (*Grammar for Grownups*)	Metaphors or analogies.

pressing the need, the greater the urgency to get this book published now!
For clarity of definition, starting with the wide end of the funnel is called
an inductive method of organization. Starting with the narrow end is
called a deductive method of organization. Read the explanations and
examples for each and select the approach that best fits your book. See
Sidebar 8-3.

The Wide End of the Funnel

Introduce the general social, political, or cultural climate as the context for
your book. Make generalizations relevant to your book's concern and support them with facts and statistics. In addition, state any problems for which

The Funnel Structure of "About the Book"

Wide End First	Narrow End First
▽ *Inductive Method*	△ *Deductive Method*
Establishes social, cultural, political or other context. Builds case for timeliness answering the question, "Why this book; why now?"	Introduces your book and its strongest feature and greatest benefit. States primary problem for which your book offers a solution and states solution.
Uses statistics, authoritative quotes and testimonials to explore context and problem or need.	Offers details about book—its features and corresponding benefits, using lists, summaries.
Points out shortcomings of existing literature. Narrows "funnel" to offer your book as the perfect solution to the needs and times.	Weaves in testimonials, case studies, and quotes. Widens "funnel" to offer the larger context— social, cultural, political or other.
Introduces your book's strongest feature and greatest reader benefit.	Uses statistics, authoritative quotes to reinforce reasons for "why this book; why now?"
Uses lists, summaries, and hints to define unique features.	Integrates larger context with your specific book.
Weaves in author credentials, competitors, audience, market, and promotion throughout section.	Same.
Ends with upbeat conclusion that emphasizes most unique contribution of your book; why it is different and/or better.	Same.

your book offers solutions. Later, narrow your discussion to your book alone, highlighting why it offers exactly the right solution at the right time.

In the examples of leads, Dr. Lipman's book about snoring is one example of beginning at the wide end of the funnel (inductive method). He doesn't start by telling us about snoring; he starts by discussing sleep, setting the general context for the book.

Literary writer Susan Lloyd's *No Pictures in My Grave* demonstrates what I mean about establishing the climate for a book.

> As we enter the 1990s, the thirst for self-knowledge is epidemic. And with it, the knowledge of other cultures and ways of living. With more affluence, it seems everyone is traveling. Not content to make 21-day package tours, as amateur anthropologists and adventurers, we seek out exotic locales in the Amazon. We climb sacred Buddhist shrines in Java, or trace the ancient footsteps of pilgrims in Spain. For many of us, it is an attempt to uncover roots, or find the humanity which unites us all as world citizens. In modern society we feel disconnected from the traditional institutions of family and community and hope that in these "lost" places we can find something lost in us.

Clearly, the author is painting in broad strokes the background for her book. She describes a current, universal need that most people have or will experience.

If you choose to begin this section with the wide end of the funnel, the inductive method of organization, choose a cultural or societal context relevant to your book. For instance, books about business could begin with discussion of the economic climate. Books on parenting could begin with a discussion of social problems and changes in the family. Introduce a problem, like Susan Lloyd's description of our "thirst for self-knowledge," how "we feel disconnected from...family and community," how we hope "we can find something lost in us."

Make sure your "About the Book" section answers the two most fundamental questions asked by any editor or agent: "Why this book?" "Why now?"

Once you introduce the climate or context for your book and introduce the problem for which your book offers a solution, then funnel down to one topic—your book. You control the readers' perspective, leading them from general to specific. Background to foreground.

About the Book, from *The Fourth Era: Energy From Space*

Last year, over 1,600 world scientists and Nobel laureates gathered to issue *A Warning to Humanity*. Their statement says, in part, that "...a great change in our stewardship of the earth and the life on it is required if vast human misery is to be avoided and our global home on this planet is not to be irretrievably mutilated." Among the actions called for is to reduce the use of fossil fuels and to increase the use of solar energy and other energy sources that are inexhaustible and environmentally benign.

"When you look closely, you find so many things going wrong with the environment. You are forced to reassess the hypothesis of intelligent life on Earth."

Astronomer Carl Sagan

Imagine a world with clean air, even in its largest cities. Imagine a world without the hazard of poisonous nuclear wastes. Imagine a world in which even the most remote jungle village has access to electricity for all of its needs. Imagine a world where the production and distribution of energy also helps to grow the food supply. Imagine a world in which oil-rich countries can't blackmail other nations. Imagine a world where the average monthly electric bill, including heating in winter, is only $30 a month. Imagine a world with quiet, affordable, nonpolluting transportation for everyone. [italics by proposal writer]

Now imagine that this scenario isn't some science fiction fantasy but a reliable representation of the world within the foreseeable future; possibly within the next twelve years according to Ralph Nansen, author of *The Fourth Era: Energy From Space....*

In the example in Sidebar 8-3, notice how space scientist Ralph Nansen accomplishes several important jobs for the first page of a section describing a book:

- Establishes the context for his book by acquainting the reader with the problem his book offers to solve.
- Uses statistics, a specific quote from a scientific paper, and a quote from a recognized scientist.

- Hooks reader interest with a powerful paragraph of promises that presumably his book fulfills.
- Narrows the funnel to introduce his book.

The Narrow End of the Funnel First

This beginning for "About the Book" boldly dominates the portrait, not allowing the eye to stray from front and center. In this method of organization, you introduce your book, at once emphasizing the promise it makes to readers and showcasing its unique features. After you've "sold" this, relax and introduce the context in society that makes your book well-timed and the problems for which your book offers a solution.

Naturopathic physician Dr. Weintraub adopted this no-nonsense, direct (deductive) approach for her section about her book, *Body Salts: The Way to Health Naturally*.

> The body is made up of cells. Different kinds of cells build up the different tissues and organs of the body. The difference in the cells is largely determined by the kind of inorganic salts that enter into their composition. If we burn the body, or any part of it, we obtain the ashes. These are the inorganic constituents of the body, the salts of iron, magnesium, lime, etc., which build up its tissues. These inorganic salts are the tissue builders, the architects of the organism, and both the structure and vitality of the body depend upon their proper quantity and distribution in every cell. The biochemical treatment uses these inorganic cell salts, when properly prepared for assimilation, and they are the tissue remedies that are used in *Body Salts—The Way to Health Naturally*.

Although one could say that Dr. Skye Weintraub began with an introduction to the nature of cells, a kind of wider-funnel idea, she is really only educating the lay reader directly on the creation of cell salts, so I consider it a narrow funnel approach. Had she begun this section with a wide funnel, I would have expected to see references to deteriorating health in our population, our need for balancing our body chemistries, and perhaps a context for the increase in public interest in natural treatments.

If you use the narrow funnel, or direct (deductive) approach, then eventually expand your focus to address the larger context for your book. Doing this supplies the needed persuasive context for your book.

THE CONCLUSION

A short, upbeat conclusion should end your "About the Book." Still generate enthusiasm, which you hope, by now, has infected the agent/editor. For instance, consider the inspirational conclusion crafted by coauthor Carolyn Cotter:

> *Stop Being Manipulated* can be read easily in a few hours. It leaves the readers with fresh ideas, tangible techniques, and hope. And with hope, everything is possible.

You may choose to end your chapter by summarizing the primary benefits to readers and reiterating your targeted audience, as did linguistics educator Rosemarie Ostler:

> *The Hidden Life of Language* provides an illuminating look at that most human of skills, our ability to use language. This book is for everyone who has ever been curious (or flummoxed, misorderly, all adrift, or just plan bumfuzzled) about their or other people's ways of talking.

Your conclusion should continue to inform, dazzle, and persuade right to the end, as did Dr. Lipman's:

> Aimed at the snorer and the "snoree," the medical waiting room and the hotel and motel night table, *The A-B-Z-Z-Z's of Snoring* finally offers snorers the possibility for silence and solace...and their long-suffering companions the opportunity to return from the spare room to the bedroom. It can't miss.

It's customary in "About the Book" to repeat the title of your "can't miss" proposed book often—at least one time per page. This may seem affected, but it is convention. In your conclusion, repeat your title one more time.

Five Categories of Information

You've already seen from the examples and Sidebar 8-3 how proposal writers include other specific types of information. For style as well as substance, make sure you also understand and include these in your "About the Book." These five categories of information include:

- Problems and Solutions;
- Benefits and Features;
- Personal Examples;
- Specifics; and
- Hint-and-tease items.

PROBLEMS AND SOLUTIONS

Before writing your rough draft of this section, make a list of the problems that your book will address. Even if you simply want to share your personal experiences, you can usually link them with a larger social issue. For her inner-journey book, Susan Lloyd created a tie between our collective thirst for self-knowledge and the individual's lack of connection with family and culture.

Some books have one clear problem they address, such as Dr. Lipman's book on snoring. After his lead where he quotes poets on sleep, he juxtaposes the non-poetic reality of snoring with a letter to Dear Abby:

Dear Abby:
I am desperately trying to find a cure for my husband's snoring. After being married for 27 years, I am convinced that there is no cure other than killing him, which is illegal in our country.

Has Dr. Lipman effectively introduced an agent/editor to the problem his book addresses? Such a personal testimony as a "Dear Abby" makes a powerful point, but Dr. Lipman continues to broaden his presentation of the problem:

Over 40 million Americans snore. [This one-line paragraph makes greater impact.]
For some, it is no more than an occasional and innocuous habit. But for many, it represents a nightly disturbance that turns that "timely dew of sleep" into a disruptive and nerve-racking experience for those with whom they share their lives.

All right, I'm convinced, snoring is a problem. Still, in his "About the Book," Dr. Lipman outlines other problems created by snoring, such as "adversely affect[ing] the quality of the snorer's waking life," and "represents a health condition serious enough to warrant medical attention." Several paragraphs later, he picks up the problem by offering a list of symptoms that could signal a snoring problem—just in case a snorer doesn't have a spouse who is ready to kill him over her lost sleep.

After nearly a page of defining, developing, and presenting the problem of snoring, Dr. Lipman introduces his book and defines, develops, and presents his solutions in equal detail.

Take time to brainstorm all the possible problems your book addresses. What solutions do you offer through your book? Write both down and decide which problem is primary and which solution, therefore, is the focus of your book.

Look back at the sample "About the Book" by business consultant Lucia H. Hedrick in Sidebar 8-1. She highlights the problem through underlining. What's her readers' problem? They want to get organized and stop floundering. They're not having much fun. What solution does her book offer? We don't really get *the solution* until near the end of her "About the Book" when she funnels down to her book specifically. But then she tells us that her book "will provide a simple, uncluttered method for getting organized, getting going and getting things done." Her title broadcasts her solution: *Five Days to an Organized Life*. If you think back to the list of slants in chapter two, you'll be able to identify her slant as a promise. The title also portrays the solution to the readers' problem in the form of a promise.

BENEFITS AND FEATURES

Benefits and features are similar to problems and solutions. If you'll recall from the discussion of concept statements, benefits describe what the reader gets from your book. They denote take-home value; your readers can implement benefits to make changes in their lives. Benefits can be tangible, like organizing your desk, stopping snoring, or writing a professional proposal. Or, they can be intangible, like gaining freedom, feeling more fulfilled, expanding understanding, or feeling more self-confident.

Features describe how a book delivers those tangible or intangible benefits. They include properties of the book, by way of structure as well as content; they are the florist's car that delivers the dozen red roses. Features include: step-by-step instructions, diagrams, interviews, examples, questions, exercises, maps, and bibliographic information.

After Dr. Derek S. Lipman finished outlining the problem of snoring, he introduced a solution by offering his book's features, which I have italicized: "The *A-B-Z-Z-Z's of Snoring* [proposal title] solves this problem of misdiagnosis by providing *easy-to-follow diagrams and flow charts* that identify and classify snoring according to degrees *and symptoms*, as well as treatment options."

Present and emphasize the most important ones first, working in the rest as you progress through "About the Book." Features tend to appear in the narrow part of the funnel. If you begin with the wide end of the funnel, inductively, features usually dominate the last part of the section, with benefits sandwiched between.

Benefits and features offer ideal material for lists. When indented and bulleted, they offer visual stimulation and relief from paragraphs. They draw interest and give a great sense that you are both organized and understand what your book really offers.

> Make a list of your book's benefits and features and rank them by importance.

If you begin with the narrow end of the funnel, benefits and features appear right away, mixed with discussion of the problem and solutions.

PERSONAL EXAMPLES

Personal examples add humanity to the discussion of your book, and make your agent/editor identify with the real or created person's story, and the problem. They give you a chance to offer parallels to your reader demographics and, in effect, bring your targeted reader to life through carefully selected personal examples or crafted anecdotes, and demonstrate how your readers' suffering will be relieved by your solutions. Personal examples lend testimony to your solutions.

Dr. Lipman's example of the letter to "Dear Abby" is a great personal example. Later, he indents and offers what I call "an up-close-and-personal" example of one of his patients, as follows:

> Jerry Hamilton, a thirty-seven-year-old fireman, didn't know the meaning of a quiet night. Neither did his coworkers...until they banished him from the firehouse to a nearby trailer, which they equipped with an alarm system. At home, Jerry's girlfriend resigned herself to sleeping in the spare room. On the rare nights that she shared his bed, she would lie in the darkness surrounded by the frightening din of his snoring...fearful of the seemingly endless periods when he appeared to stop breathing, choke, and then revive himself with huge gasps while thrashing about with his arms and legs. Their relationship deteriorated, as did Jerry's

health. He began to experience gradual loss of energy and took catnaps wherever and whenever he could.

Dr. Lipman uses this case study to tell his agent/editor about other sleep disorders for which snoring may be a symptom.

Some writers use short quotes that work as personal examples. In travel writer Susan Lloyd's proposal on *The Last Zapatista*, she offers the following sentence: "Zapata has become the *campesinos*' figurehead, role model, and inspiration. 'Zapata never died,' the people tell the author. 'He has come back!'"

You can use personal examples to "show" the problem and the solutions or benefits. Not only are they powerful because they humanize your topic, they also demonstrate professional nonfiction writing, and the ability to "show" instead of "tell."

SPECIFICS

Specifics offer dashes of color and detail that transform a mediocre though well-done "About the Book" into a spectacular one. Specifics—facts, statistics, quotes by authorities, quotes by everyday people, and examples—support general statements and bring clarity and focus. Use as many of these as you can throughout your "About the Book" and throughout your proposal.

Notice the focusing effect of facts and statistics in business consultant Lucy H. Hedrick's sample "About the Book" featured near the beginning of this chapter. Recall her specific examples, such as, "laundry in the laundry basket, pencils in the pencil box, books on the bookshelf...learn to play an instrument, to operate a computer, or to make a tasty omelet."

Because you probably have completed some preliminary research on your subject by the time you get to this section, I hope you have jotted down some dazzling facts and figures that you can now include. Here are some of the specifics I used to give a backdrop of the publishing industry:

> According to John Baker, editor of *Publishers Weekly*, "Publishing is now a 12 billion-dollar industry.... Over 50,000 titles are published each year; of them 85 percent are nonfiction." First-time authors comprise an incredible 75 percent of this group. According to Baker, writers may choose from among some 20,000 publishers, although 70 percent of all books published in the United States are produced by ten giant conglomerates.

Specifics add the excitement that keeps the agent/editor reading. Often the main distinguishing point between good amateur writing and salable professional writing is the writer's command of specifics.

HINT-AND-TEASE ITEMS

Hint-and-tease refers to tidbits about your credentials, the competition, market, production, and promotion. Just tidbits. Just enough to answer the emerging questions an agent/editor will have about each of these sections to come, but not so much that they won't feel excited and motivated to find out the full story. These hints are like coming attractions to moviegoers, just as the entire concept statement is a coming attraction for the proposal.

For instance, instead of using your book title to begin a sentence, reword it to say, "Teacher and researcher, Jane Doe offers the reader..." Now you've hinted about your author credentials. When you begin to discuss the features that make your book unique, throw in some contrasting statement about a competitive book, such as, "In contrast to Joe Smith's book on...(title) includes the latest research about..." You've now planted a tease about the section on competition.

Look for ways to hint-and-tease in "About the Book" using items drawn from each of your subsequent sections. Not only will this pique agent/editor interest, it will begin to answer questions and quell anxieties.

Style of Presentation

Think graphically, visually. Work with your words as a layout artist might. Be creative but don't overdo it. Consider putting your book's title in bold or caps, or both, rather than underlining it.

> Remember, this is your sales portrait; use your full palette: (•) bullets, indented quotes, italics, underlines, CAPS, boxes, and S P A C E .

Although the sample "About the Book" on *Five Days* used fewer "visuals" than most proposals, notice how the author did make frequent use of underlining.

Another stylistic device in "About the Book" is to offer bulleted lists. They are used to highlight the benefits to the reader, its features, or the topics that make it unique.

You will want to keep your lists powerful in content as well as in appearance. Here are five guidelines:

1. List no fewer than three items. I prefer three to five. Longer lists tend to overload the reader with the feeling they'll have to sort too much data.
2. Keep marbles and eggs in separate lists. Just benefits or just features will be clearer than benefits mixed with features.
3. Always set off your book's special qualities, or your special qualifications, in bulleted lists.
4. Keep entries short.
5. Rank the contents of your lists, giving the strongest or most important first.
6. Make lists parallel in grammatical structure; for instance, use active verbs like the ones in this list.

In the example that follows, counselor and child-development specialist Dean Walker uses a list to highlight his book's features and benefits.

> To parents who want to raise real people, *Organic Parenting* brings these benefits:
> - Explains the "set-up," or how the human condition makes it easy for children to grow into wounded adults.
> - Describes common parenting practices that "work, but wound" and links them with the legacy of "unrealness"— feelings of shame, emptiness, inequality, and unworthiness.
> - Shows parents how to make a "parenting map" that will help them lead their children to the destination of competence and confidence.
> - Illustrates the four principles of relating that provide the framework for healthy interactions with children (and other human beings).
> [Dean continues his list of five other benefits and features.]

Another stylistic element of "About the Book," perhaps even more pronounced than in the other sections, is repetition of your book title, which should also be highlighted by caps, bold, or underlining. While repetition of the title can be overdone—once every paragraph would be too much—if your title appears once or twice each page, you won't go wrong.

Last of all, it's typical for "About the Book" to span three to five single-spaced pages or twice that in double-space. This allows you plenty of

Most Common Problems in "About the Book" and Solutions to Them

Problem	Solution
1. Lacks organization—wanders all over the place.	The solution to this problem is to plan ahead and outline. Decide on an inductive method or deductive method and be clear about the problem, solution, features and benefits. Sketch an outline and then rewrite.
2. Lackluster leads.	As a showcase for your writing, "About the Book" must sustain the excitement you've generated in "The Concept Statement." You've got to put out energy, show the editor you know what a lead is, and keep selling.
3. Section too long or includes tangents. Almost reads like actual chapters.	Shorten. Outline.
4. Boring writing. Often this judgment corresponds to a lack of specifics and overuse of the to-be verb: is, was/were, be and other inactive verbs, such as seems or appears.	Shorten sentences. All but eliminate adjectives and adverbs. Use concrete nouns.
5. No clear-cut benefit. Writers sometimes get so wrapped up in the proposed book's features, they fail to mention what their readers will get from it.	Specify audience, market.
6. Overly long lists. One client had over 20 items on a bulleted list. She had brain-stormed her book's contents	In general, keep to five or less, but have several groupings, if you choose.

and put these freeassociations
down without thought to
groupings, order, parallelism,
or quantity.

7. Includes a short chapter-by-outline or table of contents in "About the Book." Since the agent/editor sees these later in the proposal, they shouldn't appear verbatim in "About the Book."

Pull out your strongest chapter points—what makes your book unique, fascinating, and worth reading and feature them.

8. No sociopolitical or cultural context. No climate.

What helps establish your book's timeliness is providing an overview of the times with regard to your subject. Establishing context or climate for your book increases urgency. Make the agent/editor believe the world needs your book ASAP.

9. No mention of author name, qualifications, competitive titles, audience, or market.

Scant mention at least serves to answer questions and hint-and-tease about sections to come.

10. Diction too high, syntax too complex for the proposal. *Academese* is the kiss of death, unless you are planning to write and sell to a university press or an academic audience.

Study writing for lay readers and emulate. Watch T.V.

opportunity to develop your topic, yet not to slip into outlining the book (that comes later). In style, this section presents the book but doesn't dissect it.

Troubleshooting

By the time you've drafted "About the Book," you've accomplished a major task. *But*, expect to rewrite and revise this section many times—after you put it away for a while. Most writers revise this section half a dozen times. After I edit a proposal, the writer usually faces several more revisions. Sidebar 8-5 shows the most common problems I see in "About the Book" and possible solutions to them. Do the best you can, then move on to the rest of the proposal. When you return to this section, with a sharpened pencil and mind, you'll see it with new eyes.

Congratulate yourself, too. You've conquered a most difficult section to write. And, with the writing of "About the Book," you're about half way done, if you don't count sample chapters. Celebrate!

Worksheet for Completing the "About the Book"

For each of the following types of leads, write one for your proposal, then choose the best: Anecdotes, Impressive Facts or Statistics, Quotes, Striking Statements, Narratives, Questions, Metaphors or Analogies.

Choose an inductive method of organization (overview narrowed to your book) or deductive method (your book expanded to an overview) to structure this section.

1. Define the reader's greatest problem that your book will address.
2. Define the strongest solution your book offers.
3. List three benefits your readers should receive, beginning with the most important.
4. List three features in your book that deliver the promised benefits.
5. Define what makes your book unique.
6. Define the context or "climate" that makes your book timely.
7. Determine what you can set off in bulleted lists, such as:
   - Reader benefits
   - Book's features
   - Topics that make your book unique
   - Any "plus" value—how your book will be the first, ways you are special or super qualified as the author
8. Choose others to profile or create several personal examples.
9. List specifics you can use in "About the Book":
   - Statistic
   - Facts
   - Quotes from current magazines
   - Quotes from experts and authorities
   - Quotes from everyday people

CHAPTER NINE

Table of Contents and Chapter Summaries: Organizing Your Book

The Concept Statement
About the Book
About the Author
About the Market
About the Competition
Production Details
About Promotion
• **Table of Contents**
• **Chapter Summaries**
Sample Chapters
The Appendix

Chapter Goal: to learn how to organize your research and ideas, and to compose a table of contents and an outline in summary form of your chapters.

The word "outline" is, for some people, like the word "plague," "internal revenue service," or "lima beans" is for other people. Still others love outlining. Outlining is simply a way of organizing your material and assuring a reader of understanding. It need not be complicated, confusing, or an object of loathing. On the other hand, without a good outline, your writing *will* go awry. The resulting cleanup edit will cost you far more time than you would have spent had you planned ahead and outlined first.

You may not have had a strong reason to outline anything you've written. Your book's table of contents is, in essence, a book outline. Chapter summaries carry through this overall plan of organization. The purpose of this chapter is to help you select an organizational plan for your book and carry it through in the chapter summaries required for the proposal. Your readers will be the ultimate benefactors of your organizational efforts.

Definition and Purpose

A table of contents lists chapters by
order of appearance, and provides
each chapter's beginning page number. An effective table of contents
provides three reader services:

> Outlining a book is more than necessity; it
> is the blueprint upon which your book—
> each chapter, each section, each paragraph—
> depends.

- Previews the book;
- Projects its contents, depth, and style; and
- Provides easy access to each section.

The "chapter outlines" that agents and editors occasionally refer to are
one and the same as "chapter summaries." Although you need not create a
paragraph-by-paragraph outline of your entire book for your proposal, the
agent/editor must see solid organization to the book as a whole, as well as
order and substance within each chapter. Think of your table of contents
as the topic outline, and chapter summaries as a series of topic sentences.

Set-up for the Table of Contents

To develop your book's ideas into a table of contents:

- Review your audience and purpose;
- Divide your research notes and ideas into groups of similar topics;
- Assign working titles to these groups; and
- Select a method of organization.

REVIEW YOUR AUDIENCE AND PURPOSE

The first steps of organizing your book are easy, if you first review your
targeted audience and original purpose in writing your book. In chapters
two and three, I discussed evaluating ideas and doing preliminary research.
Recall whether you decided the purpose of your book was to inform, to
entertain, or to persuade. Think again about your targeted reader.

DIVIDE YOUR RESEARCH NOTES AND IDEAS INTO GROUPS

After your preliminary research, you'll have some sort of files, note cards,
or jottings. Divide these into groups, putting all similar items together.

These piles form your beginning chapter divisions. If you end up with only a few groups, divide them again into smaller, same-subject units.

Chapter divisions will depend on your chosen subject matter and audience. Psychologist Dr. Kathleen N. McGuire, who proposed a book called *Moved to Tears: The Meaning and Joy in Learning to Cry*, might not have devoted the first section of her book to explaining why people cry had her targeted reader been therapists, rather than the lay public.

My purpose (to inform) and my audience (inexperienced proposal writers) determined how to divide my material into chapters. Most of the chapters in this book are organized to include one section of the proposal per chapter. How else could it be done? A different book on proposal writing with a different author's vision about audience need packs all parts of a proposal into one chapter called "The Introduction." Be clear about your audience and purpose and they will lead you to a logical method of organization.

ASSIGN WORKING TITLES TO THESE GROUPS

Assign a working title to the different groups of same topics. This becomes a potential chapter title. A phrase will do. Make a list of these titles. (While it's beyond the scope of this book to cover research methods, you may want to review this area to find your most comfortable style—computer files, sticky notes, index cards, etc.)

SELECT A METHOD OF ORGANIZATION

For me, establishing a list of working titles and thinking about an organizational blueprint for my book brought great excitement. At last, the idea I'd carried in my mind began to take form on paper. I had to resist every temptation to begin writing chapter one willy-nilly, without a good outline. You should too. Channel your excitement into your first outline, the blueprint for your entire book. You accomplish this by selecting a method of organization.

> Your chapter divisions suggest a table of contents, which in turn suggests an organizational plan for your entire book.

A glance down your list of phrases of working titles for your chapters will reveal an inherent pattern. You may see an affinity between your choice of one of the three purposes—to inform, to persuade, to entertain—and these six most common methods of organization.

- Chronological order.
- Increasing or decreasing importance or complexity.
- Order of need.
- Classification and division.
- Inductive and deductive.
- Literary order.

Different subject matter lends itself to different organization. In a job as large as writing a book, you'll need several methods within a chapter, but for clarity's sake, choose just one for your table of contents. The following explanation for each of these six methods of organization and examples based on them should help you make a final selection.

Chronological Order

Chronological order presents information based on the passage of time, usually from earlier to later. Although only a few types of nonfiction books, such as histories, biographies, or travelogues, feature chronological order, many books use chronological order in at least one chapter, for instance, in a history chapter. Activists Emily Kay and Anita Saville use chronological order in their proposal for their compelling biography of the former president of the National Organization for Women (NOW), *We'll Remember in November: Molly Yard's Gift to Women's Rights*. Beginning with Molly Yard's early childhood in China, the book progresses through time to Molly Yard's democratic-party and civil-rights activism. It chronicles the history of her leadership of NOW and beyond.

Increasing or Decreasing Order of Importance or Complexity

For the right material, this method of organization gives readers a clear understanding of a whole book's idea. For example, Cotter and Green used this pattern for their book, *Stop Being Manipulated*. From their concept statement, we learn that "...[readers] will learn five amazingly simple, increasingly potent levels for countering manipulation." This method of organization is an ideal map for their book's development.

If you believe reader understanding depends upon understanding simpler principles and information first, then you should organize your book according to an increasing order of complexity. That's what real-estate investor Mabel Armstrong did to create the table of contents for her book *The Practical Woman's Guide to Real Estate Investment*. Before the novice can learn how to buy and sell to make money, she must first cover "Setting Your Goals...," "Identifying Your Team," "Learning the Ropes," "Analyzing Properties to Purchase," etc. The author introduces more complex ideas only after the reader has been exposed to simpler concepts.

Order of Need

In this method of organization, your reader's need determines your book's outline. Perhaps your book involves step-by-step instructions. Take a moment to look at the table of contents for this book. It's organized by reader need to create a proposal, something I call "writer-up," rather than in the order presented to an agent or editor for reading, something I call "agent/editor-down." Order of need also proved to be the best outlining choice for tour escort Jan G. Jett. In *Profitable Tour Escorting*, Jett leads her readers through getting a first tour, planning it, and then leading it.

Classification and Division

You can classify your book's material using either division of a whole into the classes which comprise it, or by placing a thing into the whole of which it is a part.

Naturopathic physician Dr. Weintraub created a book that lent itself perfectly to both classification and division. The first part of her book defines the eleven cell salts. In what she labels as a "repertory," readers may look up symptoms or ailments, which are further subdivided.

Biochemist Linda Jean Shepherd chose classification and division for her thought-provoking book, *Lifting the Veil: The Feminine Face of Science*. After background chapters that define the broader classifications of "masculine principle" and "feminine principle," the author divides subsequent chapters into divisions of the "feminine principle." Thus, the reader is led through chapters about qualities defined by the author as belonging to "the feminine principle," as applied to science, chapters including: feeling, receptivity, subjectivity, egalitarianism, nurturing, cooperation, feminine intuition, and relatedness.

Inductive and Deductive

When an author's intent is to persuade readers to embrace his or her point of view, the primary organizing method should be similar to a formal argument. Because "argument" commands entire texts as a form of writing, review argument form before writing a book intended primarily to persuade. The two primary ways to organize an argument are either by inductive or deductive reasoning.

Rocket scientist Ralph Nansen chose to organize his impassioned book on space-based solar energy satellites using an inductive method of organization. Early chapters of *The Fourth Era: Energy From Space* establish the context for his book by leading the reader through existing policy and former energy "eras." Middle chapters explain how solar satellite systems and energy beams work, overcoming any reader arguments about technological limitations. Subsequent chapters argue for economic viability. Last chapters unveil Ralph Nansen's solar energy development plan and leave the reader breathless regarding the potential for space development and a renewal of the earth-based environment. Successful argument at its best.

Literary Order

A variety of nonfiction subjects can be novel-like in form, biography and personal essay among them. In such a literary form, generally an inciting incident introduces a problem that grows worse as a character seeks to solve it, culminating in a climax where the problem is resolved and the character learns something.

Two unusual members of the nonfiction family are true crime and humor. Both require the preparation of a proposal, just like any other nonfiction book. Although true crime is classified as nonfiction, because it reports on actual life events and people, its overall structure is considered literary because it resembles that of a novel. Within a chapter, however, its structure relies upon analysis, the close examination of all theories and evidence.

Humor also fits literary order better than common nonfiction methods of organization. Most humorists tell stories, real and anecdotal, organizing their material around themes—dogs, ex-husbands, parenting, growing old. Well-known examples are Bill Cosby's books, such as *Fathering* or *Turning Fifty*. The material is narrative. Both true crime and humor, like novels, convey a "message," a theme for the reader to mull over. First-time authors of either humor or true crime can save themselves the heartbreak of endless rejections by first studying fiction structure, in particular, how to craft a novel.

After reviewing these six different methods of organization, select one as your "guiding light" for the duration of writing your book. Besides providing your eventual reader with clarity, this decision inspires confidence in your book plan, within yourself, and with your prospective agent and eventual publisher. Now follow this beacon as you make firm decisions about your table of contents and begin to write chapter summaries.

Selecting and Writing the Table of Contents and Chapter Summaries

With basic decisions about the organization of the whole book, you're ready to move forward. Do the following:

- Establish a first-chapter hook;
- Rewrite working titles into chapter titles, drafting a table of contents;
- Choose subtitles or chapter descriptions;
- Find each chapter's main topics; and
- Craft topic sentences and chapter summaries.

ESTABLISH A FIRST-CHAPTER HOOK

Each of the six methods of organizing a book dictate its own starting point, such as earliest in time for chronological order, or gathering material and tools for construction in order of reader need. These natural starting points may, however, be less than exciting.

Your readers are primed to secure the *benefits* that your book offers. Background, history, or developmental information rarely delivers these coveted benefits. For some books, the most compelling chapter one will be an exploration of the problem or problems for which your book offers some solution. Then, an exploration of the problem may draw the reader in as she or he anticipates answers from the rest of the book.

> All books should start with a lead chapter that hooks reader attention.

If your table of contents is a menu, your first chapter is the appetizer. Decide what will draw your reader into the book, will whet the appetite, then review the material on leads in chapter eight. Select a chapter-one hook.

REWRITE WORKING TITLES, DRAFTING A TABLE OF CONTENTS

Study tables of contents from books similar to the one you plan to write. If you decide to vary your book's organization, chapter lengths, its style or titling, be able to justify it. Other books in the same field as yours define a norm. Deciding to be different based on whim is not sufficient.

Chapter titles, like your book title, offer one more opportunity for adding pizzazz. Some titles excite more than others. Consideration of this fact is especially vital when the subject matter for two books is otherwise identical. For serious subjects, find evocative or provocative chapter titles.

Select firm chapter titles, based on your selection of one method of organization for your book. Check your titles' grammatical structure and make sure they are parallel. Now, write your chapter titles in order, beginning with your first-chapter hook. This is your table of contents.

CHOOSE SUBTITLES AND CHAPTER DESCRIPTIONS

Not every book uses chapter subtitles or chapter descriptions. Because no set rules exist for this decision, let convention guide you. Once again, review books similar to yours.

Make sure to construct titles and subtitles that are parallel in length, grammatical structure, and style. When decorator and instructor Aline Renauld Prince first conceived her book, *Cheapskate Decorating*, her titles were a hodgepodge of nonparallel ideas. In revision, her titles and subtitles are parallel in content and charm, i.e. style, but they are not yet parallel in grammatical structure. I've marked the nonparallel titles and given corrections following the example.

1. Bed Headboards Fit for a King, Queen, or any Knight
- 2. Give Windows a Lift with Balloon Shades
3. Folding Screens That Foil Prying Eyes
4. Face-Lifted Furniture: Three Easy Ways
- 5. Uniting Furniture Orphans Through Fabric and Color
6. New Life for Old Chairs (no upholstery needed)
7. High Life for Low Tables
8. Wall Hangings That Aren't a Crime
- 9. From Old to Heirloom: Decoupage Furniture
- 10. Branching Out: A Pot, Some Limbs, and Flowers
11. Large Folding Work Table (now you see it, now you don't)

Titles corrected for parallel structure:

2. Balloon Shades That Give Windows a Lift
5. Furniture Orphans United Through Fabric and Color

9. Decoupage Furniture: From Old to Heirloom
10. A Pot, Some Limbs, and Flowers: Branching Out

A real stickler for parallel structure would ask Aline Prince to make every chapter have subtitles or use none at all.

FIND EACH CHAPTER'S MAIN TOPICS

Review your research material for a given chapter and jot down main topics. Wherever your research is too thin, or not yet begun, perform the required research or brainstorm to fill in missing information.

Weed out duplications and rank topics from most important to least and in the order you've decided for each chapter.

CRAFT TOPIC SENTENCES AND WRITE CHAPTER SUMMARIES

Chapter summaries may be written in complete sentences or in fragments that begin with an active verb. Avoid the use of Roman numerals. For instance, some active verbs I used in my chapter summaries include: *explains, suggests, defines, shows, ends with, discusses, introduces, lists, offers, details, features, draws, gives, presents, advises.*

Although editors and agents accept, "This chapter explores ...Next, this chapter relates...and, this chapter ends with...," sentences that begin with active verbs are terse and dynamic. You may use abbreviated sentences without subjects, such as, "Offers new look..." instead of "This chapter offers a new look..." Where possible, avoid repetition of the verb, "will," such as "The author will explore..." Because in most cases a writer hasn't yet written the book, nearly everything in the summary has yet to be conceived, so the reader *will* learn x, y, and z.

Summarize the topics for each chapter in *specific* terms. Include facts, figures, statistics, dates, and name terms, places, persons, and concepts.

For example, counselor Dean Walker's chapter-ten summary from his proposed book *Organic Parenting* reads as follows:

Describes and illustrates with examples the use of eight parenting tools based on the organic model of parenting through relationship. These include: unconditional love (mirroring), modeling, abiding (waiting on development to solve some problems), mutual respect, choices (both allowing them for others and asserting them for oneself, including "time away"), motivating, shaping (paying close attention when the child comes closer to appropriate behavior), and communicating.

Had Dean Walker stopped with the mention of describing eight parenting tools, without naming them, the summary would have been inadequate. As it is, he not only lists them, he also defines any that he believes the agent/editor may not understand.

Limit each chapter summary to one manuscript page, two at the most (for a complicated or lengthy chapter). Single-spaced or double-spaced summaries are a matter of personal choice, although sample chapters are always double-spaced. Writers who elaborate beyond one page risk writing the chapter rather than summarizing it. On the other hand, if you provide too brief a summary, an agent or editor might question whether your idea has enough substance to warrant book-length publication.

Troubleshooting Special Cases

- Chapter summaries for simple books
- Chapter summaries for complex books

CHAPTER SUMMARIES FOR SIMPLE BOOKS

If you're a writer who leans toward brevity in your summaries, simply return to your stacks of research material for a particular chapter and see what you might have left out. Sometimes, what you may have thought of as a discrete, but less developed, chapter might be integrated with another one. More often, an inadequate chapter summary points to a need for further research into the topics of that section. After all, most writers prepare a proposal in order to write the book. Major research looms ahead, as well as development of the basic ideas. Even so, if a particular chapter is too skimpy, for purposes of a good proposal, you'll need to do more research.

A particular case of short chapters involves the step-by-step how-to book, such as a craft book. Most of the content of each chapter is likely to be how-to directions. No complex concepts or historical backdrop. Decorator Aline Prince's book, *Cheapskate Decorating* is one such book. When the chapter content is so straightforward, the summaries can only be brief. Here is her short paragraph on her chapter two, "Balloon Shades That Give Windows a Lift":

Sidebar 9-1:
From Idea to Outline to Chapter Summaries

1. Review your purpose in writing a book and the profile of your intended reader.
2. Divide your book ideas and research notes into piles of similar topics.
3. Assign working chapter titles for these piles or files.
4. Select a method of organization to outline your book from the list of six types: chronological order, increasing or decreasing importance or complexity, order of need, classification and division, inductive and deductive, or literary order.
5. Study tables of contents in books similar to yours, and create your own to correspond with the method of organization you choose.
6. Rewrite chapter titles for subject clarity, including a first chapter that hooks reader interest.
7. If appropriate to your book, choose subtitles and descriptions. Construct titles and subtitles so they are parallel in subject, grammar, and style.
8. List topics within each chapter beginning with a carefully selected lead topic.
9. Write a chapter summary for each chapter's material.

Describes these shades and how to make and mount them. Detailed are *two styles*. Instructions included for each pattern, how to figure needed yardage, how to make the mounting and shades out of (eco)logical materials. Requires reader to use a cloth tape, do basic math, figure yardage, cut fabric, do straight line machine sewing, cut two boards, nail them and install certain screws, attach pulling rings, and tie the cords.

Actually, most of this paragraph contained padding, pleasant padding. The entirety of her chapter could have been summarized as "Describes and details two styles of balloon shades, including how to make and mount them." However, the longer description should give the agent/editor a more secure feeling that the simple tasks involved in making these shades are well within the capability of even a novice, so the "padding" serves a purpose.

CHAPTER SUMMARIES FOR COMPLEX BOOKS

Chapter summaries pose particular challenges for writers of books that are highly technical or filled with many levels of meaning. To present the details of a chapter in a technical book without swamping the reader with unknowns, consider following the example of Canadian psychologist Dr. Michael Rousell in a chapter summary for his proposed book, *Sudden Impact*. Notice how he begins his chapter-three summary, "What Is Hypnosis?" with a paragraph of explanatory prose, then shifts to an easy-to-read list.

> The Amazing Kreskin offers $100,000 to anyone who can definitively prove that there is such a thing as a discrete altered mental state called the hypnotic state. For three decades, Kreskin has successfully defended his challenge. He claims (and has frequently demonstrated to live audiences) that he can produce any so-called "hypnotic phenomenon" outside a context normally referred to as hypnosis. According to Kreskin, there is nothing extraordinary about hypnosis; it is a natural phenomenon.
>
> Chapter Three:
> - Examines hypnosis broadly from a naturalistic perspective: hypnotic phenomena as normal although uncommon.
> - Presents examples of common behaviors that become specified as *deep trance phenomena* when they appear in the context of hypnosis.
> - Reveals varied pathways (inductions) to the highly suggestible state (hypnotic state): direct, indirect, ritualized, spontaneous.
> - Explores current scientific controversies, misconceptions, myths, and apparent dangers of hypnosis.
> - Examines common, although inadvertent, uses of hypnotic conditions.
> - Describes the subjective experience of hypnosis.
> - Finishes by revealing how the typical classroom teacher has more power to influence than the traditional hypnotist.

Sidebar 9-2:

Seven Steps to Stirring Chapter Summaries

1. Avoid weak sentence starts, such as "It is" and "There is."
2. Vary sentence beginnings, as well as sentence types and lengths.
3. Minimize use of "This chapter..." and "Readers will...."
4. Select active verbs; reduce use of to-be verbs: is/was/were.
5. Include topics, terms, facts and other specifics.
6. Make sure each chapter summary includes at least one clear benefit and one specific feature.
7. Limit summaries to one page, single-spaced. (See "special cases" for exceptions.) Make sure that short summaries, one to two paragraphs, contain enough specific topics to display a well-defined chapter.

If you use a list like Dr. Rousell's, you'll resist the temptation to write your actual chapter or overwhelm the reader with detail. Dr. Rousell's introductory paragraph in the chapter summary also sends the message that the reader will encounter friendly prose, not just scientific detail.

Travel writers and personal-experience writers face a second case where complexity may pose a particular difficulty in writing succinct chapter summaries. First, they must make clear to the agent/editor what is happening in the external journey. Second, they must bring out the personal meaning of their travels. Each chapter summary must demonstrate that it supports a theme, delivers a pearl of wisdom, or offers a captivating insight to the reader. To satisfy this necessity, these authors face the job of braiding several strands into their stories. Doing so may take them into a second page for each chapter summary. Here is a small portion of the summary from chapter five, "Lucia's Kitchen, Clara's Restaurant," in Susan Lloyd's literary nonfiction book, *No Pictures In My Grave*:

> Back in Trapani, the author finds a contemporary "dark goddess" hidden in the white cloaks of propriety. She is Lucia, Carlo's mother, reminding the author of her grandmother. She is an ageless crone, cooks constantly like Carolina did, and teaches the author to make couscous. This grain staple's fertility symbolism is counterpointed by the deathlike dirge Lucia sings. She sifts the

grain while shrieking countless verses of the Madonna's lamentation. Now the author hears the song of darkness, of longing that Sicilian women sing. Though Lucia is a formidable matriarch, she is a caged bird....

Chapter summaries for personal experiences and journeys require an extra amount of finesse, because you must boil down everything into its strongest essence, blending description, action, information, and interpretation. Your goal is to convince the agent/editor that your reader will be so powerfully moved that he or she will share your insights and emotions.

CHAPTER TEN

The Heart of Your Proposal: Sample Chapters

The Concept Statement
About the Book
About the Author
About the Market
About the Competition
Production Details
About Promotion
Table of Contents
Chapter Summaries
• **Sample Chapters**
The Appendix

Chapter Goal: To select and write sample chapters that will best showcase your book and sell your proposal.

After learning how to write in the structure and style required for the proposal sections, you now get to change gears. Writing your sample chapters—or rewriting ones you've previously drafted—requires the adoption of a different mindset and style than the one you assumed for writing the proposal. In these chapters, you must make good on all your promises and claims and satisfy the anticipation you've generated by writing an exciting proposal.

Definition and Purpose

Sample chapters are carefully written and thoughtfully selected excerpts from your book. While some agents and editors accept two chapters, or occasionally even one substantial chapter, most request three sample chapters.

Well-written sample chapters convince editors that you can complete the book you propose. They follow-through on the promises you made in

"About the Book." They showcase the contribution your book offers to make in its field. Last of all, they give you have an opportunity to parade your unique style of writing, thereby proving you have the skill to craft a book—and the originality to make it interesting.

Criteria for Selection of Sample Chapters

If this is your first book, editors will expect a good chunk of writing, anywhere from 30 to 60 pages double-spaced. Put yourself behind an editor's reading glasses. Editors considering a previously unpublished author must be assured that you can finish such a big project and not drop the ball half way through. One would think editors would insist on seeing an entire book, as they do first novels. But then, in contrast to nonfiction, fiction can go awry at any point in the process regardless of a good outline. The proposal, including the chapter summaries and sample chapters, provides enough writing samples for editors to make an accurate judgment to confidently grant a contract on a nonfiction book.

Some editors prefer to see nonconsecutive sample chapters, while others like consecutive chapters. An editor with St. Martin's Press expressed a widespread preference in saying: "While the chapters don't need to be from the beginning of the book, they do need to be substantive, rather than simply introductory." In general, you should select your sample chapters to fulfill three functions:

- They should be the most representative of your originality or the unique contribution your book makes.
- They should be the chapters that best showcase your writing.
- They should include at least one chapter that would be easier to write.

Many times, chapters that capture your originality or your unique contribution are not necessarily consecutive. Introductory or first chapters rarely represent the book's originality or showcase your writing. Chapter one may be the hardest of all chapters in a book to write. In my experience, most writers consider beginnings tortuous at worst, unpleasant at best. They also require more rewriting than any other chapter. Perhaps this universal phenomena has something to do with the specter of facing a blank page, and several hundred more beyond it, at a time when your brain is stuffed full of the entire book's contents. Or, perhaps you haven't truly been able to see the organization clearly and need to spend more time outlining. Most beginnings warm the reader to the ideas and lay down foundation material, background, definitions, or history. In middle and later chapters, readers encounter the material that conveys the core of the book's message.

Autobiographies, personal-experience stories, inner journey and travel memoirs—like Susan Lloyd's—must present the same first chapters encountered by the reader. Often personal-experience stories end up structured like a novel, beginning with an inciting incident that introduces a goal and tests the character. Getting the book off to the right start is as critical in these types of nonfiction as in a novel. In these books, you must offer chapter one as a sample chapter.

> Choose to write the sample chapters that are most impressive and most representative.

Another form of insurance is to include the first two chapters, but then to write and submit one from later in your work. You orient the agent/editor to your ideas and then deliver a more complex, and original, application of them later on. And, if your book is divided into larger parts or sections, I advise showing a chapter from each section.

The best way to select sample chapters is to read through your chapter summaries. Some chapters will look easier to write but may not showcase your writing or supply the requirement mentioned by the St. Martin's editor to be "substantive." Recall the ways in which you believe your book to be better and different from others in print, and choose the chapters that are most representative of that contribution.

Writing Your Sample Chapters

Once you've selected your sample chapters, you will appreciate the outlining work you did for your table of contents and chapter summaries. The good news is that your chapter summaries represent the hardest work in producing solid, well-organized sample chapters. The bad news is that well-written sample chapters require attention to several more details. You must:

- Craft a hooking lead for each sample chapter.
- Define terms and be clear about the purpose of each paragraph, section, and chapter.

- Plant a reader payoff, a benefit, on every page.
- Rewrite and edit for clarity, conciseness, and style.

CRAFT A HOOKING LEAD FOR EACH SAMPLE CHAPTER

In chapter eight, I introduced the different types of leads you could use to begin "About the Book." These same leads can be used to begin your sample chapters.

You may recall that your sample chapters will have two types of readers. These sample chapters will be read first by agents and editors who may not be as forgiving as the second group of readers, your book's purchaser.

Because you are in a competitive situation, vying with hundreds of other authors for agent representation and then again for editorial committee selection, polish your sample chapter leads. Study books like yours and determine which chapters have obviously been crafted with knowledge of leads in mind. Decide which leads seem most powerful and best fit your material. Try several and select the best.

DEfiNE TERMS AND BE CLEAR ABOUT PURPOSE

Define terms or words used in specialized ways. It's so easy for you, the expert on your subject, to forget that the reader doesn't know, for instance, what a sidebar is! (A sidebar is a short article that accompanies the chapter, usually set off graphically on a page by itself—often boxed within the text, or otherwise distinguished.)

As you select and write each sample chapter, remember that it has a purpose, as does each section and each paragraph within it. Sometimes the content will suggest two directions—an author's purpose versus a reader's need. For instance, I've collected a stack of great proposal examples. I'd like to supply you with six of them. That's author's purpose. You, the reader, simply want to understand the point I'm making, and one example would do just fine. That's reader's need. It's a balance that must be struck in the interest of clarity. Try to cast yourself in both roles to better appreciate the problem. Then give the reader's need priority.

PLANT A READER PAYOFF, A BENEFIT, ON EVERY PAGE

Payoffs reward your reader for their effort. Payoffs are particular benefits that may or may not be the same as the ones you touted in "About the

Book." They could be anything from understanding, motivation, an instruction, an example, to a vicarious thrill.

Although one payoff per page may not be an average you maintain throughout your book, approximate it in your sample chapters for at least one good reason: sales. When you are finished rewriting your book on contract, you smooth out any differences in style. At the proposal stage, you're selling the sizzle of your book; in the sample chapters you're adding substance—your belief that you have something new, different, better than what has previously been published. Make sure your agent or editor can validate your belief on every page.

> Make sure you plant at least one payoff on every page of each sample chapter.

REWRITE AND EDIT FOR CLARITY, CONCISENESS, AND STYLE

Throughout these chapters, I've emphasized basic techniques of professional nonfiction writing. Here, in the sample chapters, the writing that you hope thousands or tens of thousands of readers will pore over, you want to present your very best writing. A strongly crafted lead gets your chapter started right. Ferret out other weaknesses in technique by reviewing books on professional nonfiction writing that are recommended in the Resource Directory. Two of my favorites are by instructor, novelist, and columnist Gary Provost—*Make Your Words Work* and *100 Ways to Improve Your Writing*. For a grammar review, try grammarian Val Dumond's *Grammar for Grownups*, mentioned throughout this book.

"Finished" is a word many writers never use. The nature of writing is such that it can always be improved. After you have written and revised your sample chapters until you can see nothing more that you can do, you're ready for editing. Once you've reached the limits of your skills to self-edit, the logical next step is to ask someone else to critically comment. Unless your nearest and dearest are writing professionals, let a qualified person outside of well-meaning family or friends critique and edit your work. A lot can be said for having your material read by someone with no vested interest.

When you are ready to hand your work over to a freelance editor, be prepared to specify what you would like that person to accomplish. Of course, you'll want your editor to do copyediting—to catch your typos and your grammar, spelling, and punctuation errors. Because poor organization tops the list of weaknesses in nonfiction writing, specifically mention this concern. To get the most help, supply chapter summaries and outlines of sample chapters.

Exceptions and Special Cases

Here are some special cases and exceptions to the guidelines laid out at the beginning of the chapter for writing your sample chapter:

- Options for previously published authors;
- Proposals that need more sample chapters;
- When to include an introduction in lieu of a sample chapter;
- What to do when you have a finished book before beginning the proposal process; and
- Handling artwork and photographs.

OPTIONS FOR PREVIOUSLY PUBLISHED AUTHORS

When you've already had a book published and are working with the same agent, you *may* be able to submit a proposal without sample chapters. There are some rewards in a writer's life! In fact, you may be able to get by with an abbreviated form of the proposal that hits the highlights of each section but offers much less detail. Why? Because you've demonstrated your ability to write and presumably have one or more successes to your credit. Regardless, be prepared for the possibility that a new publisher—not the one who published your prior book—may still require a full proposal.

PROPOSALS THAT NEED MORE SAMPLE CHAPTERS

Some editors believe that two chapters are enough to demonstrate writing ability and more won't make a difference. However, agents or editors may request that you produce additional chapters, if the samples you present are short, and if they feel unsure of your writing skill. This holds true especially for a writer whose qualifications might appear thin and who lacks publishing credits.

For instance, I'm working with a psychologist who is writing a self-help book. John's got solid credentials as a therapist, but no publishing credits and no history of public appearances. He's been quietly doing a great job with people for years and years. Now he wants to go public. He's never written articles. He lacks what agent Denise Marcil calls "national outreach," meaning a record of television appearances, radio shows, and seminars and workshops. Even if John writes a third or fourth sample chapter, he is unlikely to secure interest with a major publisher. Instead, his first book probably will find a home with a small to mid-sized publisher until he gains name recognition.

If you fall into a similar situation, don't wait for an agent to tell you to write a third chapter. You may simply get rejected, never knowing if more exposure to your writing and your book would have made the difference. You may also benefit through increased skill and confidence by writing more of your book. John had to write a rough draft of his entire book simply to learn how to write for the general reader.

WHEN TO INCLUDE AN INTRODUCTION IN LIEU OF A SAMPLE CHAPTER

Often, introductions explain where authors received the inspiration for their books. They may elucidate philosophies about the material and give quick overviews of the contents. Frequently, they tell the reader how to best use a book. In other words, they offer introductory thoughts. Generally, an introduction should not be selected as a sample chapter.

If, however, your introduction begins with foundation material, and offers theories upon which the rest of the book depends, your introduction may be necessary for an agent/editor to grasp your ideas. Then, you must offer the introduction as one sample chapter and probably chapter one as another. Perhaps, though, you should consider renumbering your chapters and call your present introduction "chapter one."

WHAT TO DO WHEN YOU HAVE A FINISHED BOOK BEFORE BEGINNING THE PROPOSAL PROCESS

My heart sinks when I get calls from writers who have been slaving away without knowing the "rules" of publishing. "I've spent three years writing my book," the writer might say. "I'm ready to get it published. Can you tell me whether I should send it to an agent first or to a publisher directly?"

If you have finished your book, you have the luxury of really knowing your material, having worked out changes and bugs from the original vision. The "however" implied here is that you must still write a proposal, and your proposal will only include two or three sample chapters. No one wants you to send your entire manuscript—with a few rare exceptions. If you have an "in"—let's say your brother-in-law is an editorial assistant at Scribners—well, maybe he'll read the book or get it to the correct reader. Maybe you're dating an agent and she says she'll read the whole book. If you can't lasso an exception, then put the book aside, write a proposal, and select your best chapters to include as samples.

HANDLING ARTWORK AND PHOTOGRAPHY

If your book includes illustrations or photos created by an artist whose contribution you deem important, then you should also submit samples of his or her work. If you have illustrated your sample chapters, or purchased artwork or photography for your sample chapters, include samples of these works—whether or not you share co-authorship with the artist.

Submit copies (don't send originals) of illustrations on 8 $\frac{1}{2}$" x 11" paper, and label where they belong in the text. When you reach the place in your sample chapter where an illustration would be, simply type a code, such as "illustration #1, or A." Then include the illustration page after the text where it would appear. An additional clue to where the illustration would appear is the page number of the illustration. Make sure it is the *same* page number as the page of text. If you have more than one illustration (or photo) per page, you can go down the alphabet to label each one, page number plus a letter, such as 52a, 52b, 52c to indicate three different illustrations all appearing on page 52 in the text. If your illustration would contain a caption when printed, for submission, make sure you type this underneath the illustration.

For color artwork and most photographs, submission of laser photocopies is fine. If you intend to include black-and-white photography, it's up to you whether you believe laser copies are sufficient, or whether you prefer the more traditional 8" x 10" glossies. For slides, buy the kind of insert that allows you to slip them into pockets, often 20 to a sheet. On a paper behind the slides, include identification and caption details. The slides and the caption sheet are usually packaged in a folder pocket that holds the entire proposal, or at the end of the sample chapters.

If your artwork is something you generate with your computer program, some form of line drawings, graphs, tables, or figures, you can probably include these items in sequence within your text. If you're not able to integrate them in your text, put the text first and the artwork on the page that follows, as indicated earlier in the chapter.

Once you've selected and written your sample chapters, revised them to the best of your ability, and shipped them off to a friend or editor for more input, forget about your chapters. Use the time to zero in on writing the remaining sections of the proposal covered in the next several chapters.

CHAPTER ELEVEN

Production Details: If You Had Your Way...

The Concept Statement
About the Book
About the Author
About the Market
About the Competition
• **Production Details**
About Promotion
Table of Contents
Chapter Summaries
Sample Chapters
The Appendix

Chapter Goal: To specify your requirements and preferences about your book's format, production, and delivery.

By now, you should have a clear idea about how you want your book to look and feel in its finished form. This is the section in the proposal where you translate wishes into specifications. Not that you can expect to get exactly what you wish. Although publishers have more to say about how your book is produced than you do, in "Production Details" you get to share your ideas.

Definition and Purpose

Simply expressed, this section of the proposal gives the physical specifications of your book. It lists everything you will include in addition to the text, information that helps the publisher estimate production costs and a retail price. How much your book will cost is a critical factor in whether a publisher will make an offer—and in determining the size of an advance.

From a writer's point of view, "Production Details" clarifies your vision of the whole, commits you to a delivery deadline, and gives you a chance to articulate how you would like your book to look in its finished form.

A Sample "Production Details"

This section of the proposal differs widely from author to author. It may be as short as a paragraph or as long as two pages. For a typical example, I've chosen Dr. Lipman's "Production Details" for his book on snoring.

Style

As you can see by Dr. Lipman's example, the style of this section departs from the narrative style of the rest of the proposal. A list replaces para-

---

Sidebar 11-1:
Sample: Production Details

Length:	30–35,000 words
Delivery:	6 months following delivery of first advance installment
Illustrations:	25-30, b&w
Sidebars:	5–6
Permissions:	Being sought for material in Chapters 1 & 7 (see enclosed letter)
Front matter:	Foreword offered by Melvin Belli, attorney (had UPPP operation; see enclosed letter)
Introduction:	Offered by Jack Gluckman, M.D.
	— Professor of Otolaryngology and Director of the Head and Neck Surgery Service, University of Cincinnati
	— Examiner for American Board of Otolaryngology
	— Author/coauthor of numerous medical articles and textbooks
Back matter:	Appendix: names/addresses of U.S. sleep centers
Bibliography	
Index	

---

graphs. Sentence fragments are used more often than complete sentences. The typical order of information is: length and other format ideas, delivery date, front matter, back matter, and then anything unique to your book not covered by these categories.

List and Explanation of Parts

At most, your "Production Details" will include eleven different parts or items. If listing three is all your book requires, your "Production Details" might be as simple as instructor Val Dumond's for *Grammar For Grownups*:

> The proposed book is already researched, tested and ready for writing. The manuscript could be completed in about four months. The author will be free to begin about June 1.
>
> Book length will be about 200 pages, divided into three sections:
> Section 1, Parts of Speech (75 pages);
> Section 2, Punctuation (75 pages);
> Section 3, Style (50 pages).

She chose to depart from the list style most common to this section, but she got her information across effectively.

Select from the following list of eleven possible specifications, including only those that apply directly to your project.

- Length
- Delivery date
- Computer system
- Format
- Sidebars
- Permissions
- Front matter
- Back matter
- Photographs and Artwork
- Endorsements
- Resources needed to complete your book

LENGTH

Since you haven't written your entire book, how can you know how long it will be? Make an educated guess. It has to be a fairly reasonable one, because you could be held to it.

Your best gauge for total length is the average length of your sample chapters multiplied by the number of chapters you decided upon in your table of contents. To fine-tune your estimate, reread your chapter summaries and decide whether some chapters might be longer or shorter than your sample-chapter average. If so, make an adjustment to your estimate.

Agents and editors prefer estimates that are a rounded-off number of manuscript pages, versus final printed pages (about which you cannot know). Most authors give a range within 25 pages, such as 250–275 pages or 200–225 pages. Authors who have already written their books may give the word count from their computers, rounded off, such as 65,000 words.

Even though you don't really know if your book will end up within the range you project, you must express a firm figure. Part of this goes back to sales. You want to convey confidence and certainty. After all, you are the authority on your book. Therefore, make a calculated guess based upon the standard 250 words per double-spaced page.

DELIVERY DATE

If, at the time you market your proposal, you truly have a finished, polished manuscript, put "upon receipt of advance." If you're half done, or one third done, you can make an estimate based on the time it has already taken you and on the demands in your life.

Delivery dates are typically expressed in three-month increments: 3, 6, 9, 12, or 15 months. If you've only written your sample chapters, don't commit to a delivery date earlier than 9 months. In general, even short books require months to write and rewrite. Don't cut yourself short. On the other hand, publishers don't favor dates beyond 12 to 15 months, because many acquire books to fit into publishing slots within 12 to 15 months from the date of acquisition.

In contrast, smaller publishers may be able to publish within six months of acquisition and would prefer delivery as soon as possible. Unhampered by bureaucracy, smaller publishers can get your work into print more quickly.

> Ultimately, specify what delivery date you can reasonably and comfortably fulfill.

COMPUTER SYSTEM

You can expect more and more publishers to request this information. Coauthor Carolyn Cotter's proposal was another short one, but she included this electronic information. Her "Production Details" reads as follows:

> Delivery: The book is available upon request.
> Approximate Words: 32,000
> Produced with WordPerfect 5.0. Available on 3.5-inch or 5.25-inch disk. Electronic transfer is available via modem....

Small and regional publishers especially have been quick to incorporate computers as an integral part of their production.

FORMAT

Format refers to a preferred size of book and its binding. Most writers don't include this in their "Production Details," because publishers decide, if not control, this decision. However, there is no reason not to express your vision for the book. For her book *The Last Zapatista*, Susan Lloyd created a section called "Format," as follows:

> FORMAT
> Size: 6" x 9"
> Pages: 290
> HARDBACK/TRADE PAPERBACK: Prefer the book to
> be published both in hardback and quality trade paper-
> back.

If your book includes large photographs or special charts, it may need a specific size or binding, so make sure and specify this in format.

SIDEBARS

Sidebars, those short articles that supplement a chapter, sometimes involve production set-up for graphics, for instance, to enclose in a box or to shade with a shadow or other effect. Sidebars may add production time, which translates into additional production cost. State or estimate the number of sidebars you anticipate. In the proposal for this book, for instance, I created a heading for sidebars and estimated 10 to 15.

PERMISSIONS

When you use other people's printed or published material or the essence of their original ideas, you must give them credit in your book. Credit means quoting or paraphrasing their words and giving attribution, that is, citing their name as author. You may do this in the text, in a footnote, or in a bibliography.

For small amounts of credited material, the "fair use" language of the Copyright Act states that certain uses without permission (but with attribution) are legal. The criteria are: nature of use (commercial or noncommercial), proprotion of work used, and whether or not the use denies of the holder sales.

> Your agent, and later your editor, can help you decide if you must seek formal permission to use someone else's material.

In other words, the "fair use" language is sufficiently vague to keep lawyers steadily employed.

If you are fairly certain that you will need to ask permission of others to use their words (or photos, or illustrations), then you must do the following:

- Send a permissions form to the author; and
- Develop a permissions section in "Production Details."

Send a Permissions Form

The *Chicago Manual of Style*, a reference book available in most libraries, includes a standard form for requesting permission to reprint published material. Or, you may create your own. I synthesized several permissions forms to match my needs on various projects. Because the proposal examples used in this book represent copyrighted material belonging to their creators, I was legally bound to request permission from every author whose proposal I used. The form I ended up with is included in the Sidebar 11-2. Use or adapt it to your needs; you have my permission.

If you are writing autobiography, biography, or expose, you will probably need to have permission to write about other individuals. Although I recommend that you consult with your agent, editor, and possibly an attorney, you'll find another permission form in the appendix that you may use or adapt.

Because these forms can sound intimidating to the recipient, always include a friendly cover letter that explains your book, indicates why you

Sidebar 11-2:

Permissions Form

I am preparing a book tentatively entitled *Nonfiction Book Proposals Anybody Can Write*, which Blue Heron (Hillsboro, Oregon) is planning to publish in the summer of 1995.

Please give me permission to reproduce the material listed below in any or all editions of the book, or in any part thereof and in any and all derivative works based thereon throughout the world, and in the advertising, promotion, and publicity thereof. Full credit will be given in the form of your name as author and copyright holder, title of your book, and publisher or agent, whichever is appropriate.

Please grant permission for use of excerpts from your proposal with the working title of:

Proposal Copyright (c) 19 _____ by _____
                                        Copyright Holder
All rights reserved.

Your signature above and below on this form, returned to me as soon as possible will be greatly appreciated.

Signed: _____ Dated: _____

---

need permission, and gives your timetable. Enclose a self-addressed, stamped envelope (SASE). Follow-up with a thank-you note.

Develop a Permissions Section

Here's how linguistics educator Rosemarie Ostler entered her request for permissions in her "Production Details."

> Permissions: To be obtained from Derek Bickerton (*The Roots of Language*) and Susan Curtiss (*Genie: A Psycholinguistic Study of a Modern Day 'Wild Child'*) for presentation of their original data and theories. Payments to range from $0 to $xxx for each.

Some authors ask payment, usually in the form of a flat fee, for use of their material. Others are happy to be credited, satisfied with the compliment and the increased exposure for their books and names. Generally speaking, the more famous the author or quote, the more likely it is you will have to pay a fee. While you cannot know ahead of time how much you may have to pay, the proposal process demands you put down something. If permissions cost you $500 per author or more, they will take a bite from your advance, so weigh this against the advantages of using the material.

FRONT MATTER

Front matter includes everything that goes in the front of a book. It begins with the half-title page, title page, copyright page, and table(s) of contents. The parts you need to list in your proposal are the preface, foreword, and introduction. You may also plan a dedication and acknowledgments, but they require no special mention in "Production Details." You may also choose not to have any front matter. It's unlikely that your book will include everything on the list of front matter, although comparing yours to other books like it will give you a model.

Preface

A preface is the same as an introduction, only shorter. Both are ordinarily written by the author and generally tell why and how the book was written.

Foreword

A foreword (check your spelling; it's not the same as forward) contains short introductory remarks but is written by an authority your readers will respect—usually not your mother. The idea is to have this person say kind and exciting things about your book to whet the reader's appetite and snare a sale at the bookstore. If you can line up a recognized authority in your field, a published author, or a celebrity, state this in "Production Details." Sometimes you have to pay a fee to this person; if so, note that here or under a later itemization of your expenses.

Notice in the sample "Production Details" how Dr. Lipman let the editors know they could count on the famous attorney, Melvin Belli, for a foreword. Here's how mythologist and counselor Demetra George listed her only front matter:

> Foreword: Written by Vicki Noble, author of *Motherpeace* and *The Shakti Woman*

If you haven't yet contacted authorities to write your foreword—or to provide you with a few superlatives as an endorsement—then indicate that you intend to pursue their services. Make sure to state the expertise for which these people are known. Avoid making a long wish list. It begins to look like a fishing trip, rather than a carefully selected list of individuals who really might respond positively to your request.

Introductions

If you are writing an introductory chapter to your book, you would not list it in "Production Details." Instead, include it in your chapter summaries.

Although authors usually write introductions while VIP's write forewords, introductions may be written by luminaries other than you, and should then be mentioned in "Production Details." The person need not be a household name or even known by your readers. Nevertheless, this person should have some authority to lend importance and an endorsement to your book. In the sample "Production Details," Dr. Lipman's choice of individuals to write his introduction offers a good example. Dr. Gluckman is a stranger to us, but as a medical doctor, his comments reflect what is called "warranty," a seal of approval, to the author's ideas. His credentials and words of praise will increase some readers' respect for the book even *before* they begin to read it.

BACK MATTER

When your reader finishes your last page of text, what remains is called back matter. You might want to include a bibliography, appendices, glossary, or index. Less commonly, you could have an addendum (for late, additional information), author's notes, an afterword, or a colophon (giving details about type style, design, kind of paper, and other production details).

PHOTOGRAPHS AND ARTWORK

If you plan artwork or photographs other than what is included in your word-processing program, list them under "Production Details." Photographic reproduction adds to a book's costs, color much more so than black-and-white. If your book demands "plates" for the photographs, the cost can run even higher. For example, a coffee-table book with dozens of color photographs may retail at $35–50 per book or more. You must supply the publisher with sufficient information to create an accurate budget.

Because Susan Lloyd is a professional photographer and teaches photography, photographs are an important addition to her books. For her book *The Last Zapatista*, she detailed exactly how many, what kind, and what placement she envisioned for the photographs in her book, as follows:

> Photographs
>
> Approximately ten black-and-white photographs, printed full-frame and appearing on the title page of each new chapter. Each photograph, made by the author who is a professional photographer, will illustrate the theme of the particular chapter: for instance, a photograph of Diego Rivera's mural at Chapingo, depicting Zapata buried in the ground with corn sprouting from his body (Chapter 1); a portrait of Ana Maria Zapata, in her home surrounded by memorabilia and photographs of Emiliano Zapata (Chapter 2); an image of campesino bull-riders (Chapter 3); the Zapata family at Cuahuixtla hacienda ruins (Chapter 4); a portrait of Martin Balderrama holding his young son (Chapter 5); a portrait of Emeterio Pantaleon husking corn in his adobe hut (Chapter 6), etc.

You need not go into such specific detail (I would have placed her "etc." after Chapter 3); however, such detail leaves no room for confusion about her preferences.

ENDORSEMENTS

If you do not lump your list of endorsement hopefuls in with your foreword and front matter, then list them as a separate item. Under "endorsements" list anyone whom you can guarantee (because you have spoken with them). Also list those persons whom you "plan to contact," or from whom you "hope to secure" endorsements. Don't forget to indicate their connection to your book, or how they are known.

RESOURCES NEEDED TO COMPLETE YOUR BOOK

While every book costs you money to write by way of paper, printer supplies, postage, and general office overhead, these are costs you're expected to absorb or deduct from your advance or future royalties. When completion of your book necessitates expenses beyond these usual ones, add a budget of these projected expenses to your "Production Details." You could gain a greater advance *if* the publisher is willing to cover some of your expenses—always a matter for negotiation. The primary areas that may produce additional costs are travel expenses, photographic supplies and development, long-distance telephone calls, permissions, editing, endorsements and forewords, and professional typing.

When listing expenses, round off figures and begin with the most costly item first. Here is Susan Lloyd's "Resources Needed to Complete Book" for her proposal on *No Pictures in my Grave*:

> Research for the book has been completed and four chapters have been written. I would like to utilize a residence grant I have received from the Wurlitzer Foundation in Taos, New Mexico for a three-month stay (use of writing studio) during May–July, 1991, to work on the remaining chapters. The manuscript will be finished and delivered nine months after receipt of an advance.
>
> Itemized resources are:
>
> | | |
> |---|---|
> | Travel & Board in New Mexico | $2,700 |
> | Payment for Foreword | 750 |
> | Clerical Expenses | 800 |
> | Editing | 500 |
> | Photographic Printing Supplies | 300 |
> | (if photographs are used) | |
> | Total | $5,000 |

Be prepared for the possibility that your advance may not cover all the expenses that you'll incur. Advances are not based upon your expenses, even though the philosophy behind them is to provide monies for completion of the book. You may recall that the advance is, in part, based on a formula: Retail cost of book times number of books in the print run times author's royalty percentage. On this subject, an editor at St. Martin's Press expressed his ambivalence about itemized expenses as follows:

> I often feel that the writer itemizing expenses is positioning

me. My job is to pay an advance that reflects what the publisher thinks the book is worth; that number is based on a projection of earned royalties, not on the author's expenses.

A Summary of "Production Details"

The "Production Details" section of a proposal is where the author lists specifications and preferences for the book's physical look and layout. From these details, the publisher estimates costs, including the advance, and learns when the author can deliver the finished manuscript.

Make sure your "Production Details" section includes the following:

1. Book length—rounded off in double-spaced manuscript pages or in word count.
2. Delivery date—usually expressed as "upon receipt of advance," or "in 3 months, 6 months, 9 months, 12 months, or 15 months."
3. Type of computer and word-processing program.
4. Format—if any special preferences in size, binding, treatment of text.
5. Sidebars—estimated number.
6. Permissions—how many you will seek, sometimes naming the cited authors, and indicate actual or estimated fees.
7. Front matter—whether you plan to have a preface, foreword, introduction, dedication, or acknowledgments.
8. Back matter—indicate whether you plan to have an index, bibliography, a resource directory, glossary, or appendices.
9. Photographs and artwork—details about types and any special treatments of photos or artwork.
10. Endorsements—who you've arranged or hope to contact for endorsements.
11. Resources needed to complete your book—itemized expenses, such as: travel, photographic supplies, long-distance calls, permissions, foreword fee, editing, or professional typing.

Every publisher is as different as every book deal. Many factors other than "projected earned royalties" can weigh in the awarding of an advance, such as the financial condition of the publisher, production costs versus retail price, the perceived selling power of the book, the author's reputation, the skill of your agent, and how much excitement your proposal engenders in the editor and the committee.

CHAPTER TWELVE

About Promotion: Good Morning, Springfield. Good Morning, America

Chapter Goal: To outline a workable plan for promoting your book.

When you watch Oprah, Geraldo, or Jenny Jones, you may begin to imagine yourself on their shows, answering questions about your book for an audience of millions. You may imagine what it will be like when your publisher sends you on a coast-to-coast promotional tour, all expenses paid. You may even think of the crowds, the book signings, the motels, perhaps even the chance to see Aunt Betty in Dallas whom you haven't talked to in fifteen years.

You're dreaming.

I won't deny that your book *could* be high-zoot enough to warrant this kind of treatment, all at the publisher's expense. If so, they'll call you, *they* being the publicity department of your publisher. However, a high-rolling media blitz is reserved for relatively few authors and even fewer first-time authors.

In general, publishers have suffered more than a decade of belt-tightening. Most have jettisoned promotion of what they call "midlist" books.

"Midlist" refers to those books that are not bestsellers; they may or may not earn back the monies paid in advance to the author. They are books that few people recognize by name, yet they comprise the largest number of titles in a publisher's catalog—the big hump in the bell-shaped curve.

Even though a percentage of the production costs for your book is earmarked for promotion, publishers are not obligated to spend that money on *your* book. If they have a hot title that begins to soar in sales, they can and will draw from the general promotion slush fund comprised of monies from all of their titles, to promote the hot seller.

> Make sure you have a strong plan to promote your book, and you'll be more likely to secure publisher assistance.

The sales and publicity members of the editorial committee have powerful voices in the selection of books. No matter how much an acquisitions editor loves your book, if someone in sales or publicity can make a convincing case why your book would be hard to sell, then this no vote will override the editor's yes vote.

Where are you in this picture? You had better have a strong plan to promote your own book. As literary agent Denise Marcil commented, "This is the most important part of the proposal; the more details the better."

Your efforts as the author may make the difference between your publisher soaring into the black or plunging into the red. In some cases, what you offer in "About Promotion" may make the difference between a contract offered and a proposal declined. Be specific and get the committee to believe in you as well as in your book. Offer a credible plan that demonstrates your marketing ability and willingness. Show how you will devote hours and days of your own time to help sell your book, or state your intent to hire someone else. When you propose your next book, you'll have a sales history that will make all the difference.

Definition and Purpose

Promotion refers to what you do to create sales for your book. *Publicity* is what you get for your promotional efforts, all the better if it doesn't cost you or the publisher a dime. *Advertising* is promotion that someone pays for. The best marketing plan is one that yields maximum publicity for minimal time or money. Having a lot of money for promotion helps, but does not guarantee lots of publicity or sales. Sometimes writers think advertising is the answer to selling more books. There is much debate over the utility of ads, since it is usually difficult to assess results and the origins of bookstore orders are unavailable.

Successful marketing requires knowledge and skill. In the "About Promotion" section you must demonstrate that combination—or demonstrate the willingness to learn. The agent/editor will read this section for three purposes:

- To assess your willingness, enthusiasm, and cooperative attitude toward promoting your book;
- To evaluate your connections, and therefore how many sales you might be able to generate; and
- To provide the promotion department with ideas how best to reach the market for your particular book.

Sidebar 12-1
Sample: About Promotion

PUBLICITY

There exist three major ways that the author can help to promote *Mysteries of the Dark Moon*: 1) by presenting lectures and workshops, 2) by writing magazine articles and arranging for book reviews, and 3) through media appearances.

The author, Demetra George, can promote *Mysteries of the Dark Moon* at the many workshops she presents across the United States and Canada on mythology, astrology and woman's issues. She is a popular speaker in the woman's spirituality community, and teaches on a regular basis in the San Francisco Bay Area. She has been invited to present the *Mysteries of the Dark Moon* teachings in Australia and New Zealand in January–February 1990.

She will commit to presenting one to two workshops per month in the six months following publication of *Mysteries of the Dark Moon*. Some possible places for presentations are the Omega Institute and the Open Door Center in New York, Joy Lake in Nevada, Breitenbush Retreat Center in Oregon, the Feathered Pipe Ranch in Montana, Woman's Alliance Summer Camps in California and Maine, School of Shamanic Healing Arts in Berkeley, and individual sponsoring organizations.

continued

No one cares about your book's success as strongly as you do. You know idiosyncratic ways that you can help promote your book. You must inform the publisher of these ways. The promotional section in Sidebar 12-1 by mythologist and counselor Demetra George is a particularly well-written example.

Structure and Content

STRUCTURE

Like most proposal sections, "About Promotion" should have a lead, a body, and a conclusion. Your lead should indicate your willingness to help promote your book. Be enthusiastic; sell yourself. In her promotion section,

---

Magazine articles and book reviews are a powerful way of informing the public about new publications. Magazine articles on Mysteries of the Dark Moon have appeared in *Woman of Power* and *Snake* magazines. Additional articles and book reviews can be arranged with new age magazines such as *New Age Journal*, *East-West*, *Magical Blend*, *Shaman's Drum*, *New Realities*; women's journals such as *Woman of Power*, *Snake Power*, *Circle Network News*, *Seattle Feminist Times*; and psychology journals such as *Psychology Today* and *Brain-Mind Bulletin*.

Media appearances on television and radio talk shows is by far the most powerful way of reaching large numbers of people with whom to share the Mysteries of the Dark Moon insights.

Ms. George has appeared on several television and radio programs discussing her two previous books, which include *AM Northwest*—a Portland TV talk show, *Quest Four*—a Los Angeles metaphysical interview TV show, and *Woman's Magazine*—KPFA San Francisco radio program. She has been requested to film a one-hour interview on Mysteries of the Dark Moon for a LA cable TV series entitled *The Goddess in Art* with Starr Goode.

Return visits with the above programs can be arranged. With the help of a publicist, many other interviews on radio talk programs and possibly television talk shows like Sally Jessy Raphael would greatly enhance the popularity of the book.

---

literary nonfiction writer Susan Lloyd wrote a first sentence showing her willingness and cooperative spirit: "I hope to work closely with the sales and publicity team of the publisher of..."

In the body of your "About Promotion," you can use Demetra George's example as a model. Use either third person or first person. You may also use a numbered list, rather than paragraphs. Make your "About Promotion" graphically appealing. For instance, I would have preferred bold or underlined headings to match Demetra George's numbered three ways to promote her book. Remember that agents and editors are busy, overworked, and fatigued. They have hundreds of other proposals they could be reading. Make their job easier. Organize your material well and make it visually appealing.

An entirely different way to structure the body of your promotion section is geographically.

Organization by Geography

You may use geographic headings, such as "local," "regional," and "national." The advantage of this method of organization is that you can go into detail about what you're willing to do. Since one would assume you can do your greatest promotion locally, this system can be advantageous for a writer who doesn't yet have experience in lecturing, many publishing credits, or media connections. The disadvantage is that you can end up repeating how you'll present and teach, write, or make media appearances under each heading.

You may remember counselor Dean Walker's promotion section mentioned earlier. It was organized by region. Here's another example with geographic headings written by teacher, psychologist, and hypnotist Dr. Rousell for his proposed book *Sudden Impact: Spontaneous Events That Shape Children's Lives*.

REGIONAL

In Edmonton, Alberta, Canada, a community of half a million, I am widely known as a psychologist and teacher. I will be sure that teacher and psychologist newsletters print announcements of the book's publication. Because of the controversial nature of this topic, I am certain to be a popular guest on local radio, newspaper, and TV interviews. Additionally, I will use news releases and personal contacts to offer myself as a speaker, particularly at local colleges and the university.

I am a member of the Alberta Provincial Teachers' Association and the Psychologists' Association of Alberta. I will be sure to release news of the book's publication in the regional magazines and newsletters. I will try to secure book reviews and presentations in these regional publications. Additionally, through minimal publisher financial assistance, I can organize my own regional publicity tour to ten separate teacher association zones in this province. Each zone has a mandatory teachers' convention: these conventions reach more than 12,000 teachers. I was a successful presenter with this organization in the past....

Finish your promotion section with a conclusion that reiterates the same enthusiasm and willingness to work that you projected in your lead.

CONTENT

In "About the Market," you listed possible markets for your book. Although you can expect your publisher to pursue usual channels to distribute your book to bookstores and libraries, it's a good idea to remind the publisher of specific markets known only to you.

Markets

In review, the most common markets for any book are:

- Bookstores;
- Specialty bookstores—such as religious, feminist, or travel;
- Institutional sales—such as course adoptions and direct mail to teachers, in addition to library sales;
- Special sales—such as cultural centers, museums, retail shops; and
- Subsidiary sales—such as book clubs and movies.

In "About Promotion," don't simply repeat the same markets that you itemized in "About the Market." Now go into detail. Add specifics. For example, linguistics educator Rosemarie Ostler's third paragraph of her "About Promotion" for *The Hidden Life of Language* reads as follows:

This book will sell well to libraries, so I would expect the publisher to promote book reviews in journals such as *Kirkus*, *Publishers Weekly*, *Choice*, and *Library Journal*. As a general interest book, it is also suitable for sale through book clubs.

While Rosemarie Ostler did well to suggest specific journals for review, she would have done better to have suggested specific book clubs as well. (You can find book clubs listed in *The Literary Market Place*.) Later, Rosemarie Ostler does make the specific suggestion, "Direct mailing of flyers to Linguistics and English teachers at universities should greatly increase the possibility of its being adopted for classroom use."

> Give specific names, locations, contact persons, and numbers involved when you recommend markets for your book and methods of promoting it.

After briefly reviewing the markets for your book, shift your focus to show how you can help promote it. The following section should help you organize your thoughts and develop your resources.

Promotion

In mythologist Demetra George's sample, she identified three ways any writer can promote a book and then discussed in turn how she would do each one. Adding a fourth category, I label these types as:

- Presenting and teaching;
- Writing;
- Making media appearances; and
- Using publicists.

PRESENTING AND TEACHING

Think of clubs, organizations, schools, universities, or conferences where you could teach or make presentations. I'm not talking about being a keynote speaker. Instead, presenting and teaching involves giving lectures, leading workshops, or facilitating seminars on the subject of your book. Ask your reference librarian for help in finding specific school programs, lecture series, and appropriate organization names. For a listing of 7500 conferences, look through *National Trade and Professional Associations of the United States*—or select from the 20,000 listings in the *Encyclopedia of Associations*. Quote several good matches to your book's subject. Don't overlook your own organizational memberships and affiliations. For his book on parenting, counselor Dean Walker writes:

> My membership and participation in the Oregon Counseling Association (OCA) represents a considerable potential market for my book. Last October, the annual OCA conference drew over one thousand counselors and therapists from all over Oregon. I

would market the book there from an exhibit stand to promote sales and visibility.

The Oregon School Counselors Association (OSCA), to which I also belong, drew to its spring conference in 1992 almost 500 school counselors and school psychologists from all over Oregon. This setting offers a fine opportunity for promotion of my book....

The more specific you can be in your suggestions, the more you will be able to convince a publisher that you can, in fact, help with your book's promotion.

WRITING

You can promote your book by writing book reviews, articles, flyers, and pitch letters. Pitch letters are letters whose purpose is to persuade someone to buy your product—your book—or use your services—as a lecturer, for instance. Most of your promotional writing will be aimed at newspapers, newsletters, magazines, and direct mailing.

Author Demetra George mentioned by name thirteen possible magazines or journals where she would pursue publication of magazine articles and book reviews. Notice how educator Rosemarie Ostler suggested that a direct-mail flyer be sent to Linguistic and English departments of colleges and universities.

Make an inventory of your own subscriptions, memberships, and prior publishing successes and come up with specific people to whom you can send material or media outlets where you can seek book reviews. If you can't name names, then be specific in a general way, like author Susan Lloyd did in this section of her "About Promotion" on her book *The Last Zapatista*:

> ...I will also be able to utilize numerous connections I have in the Latino community—a growing force in the southern Oregon area. Venues in the area include three Spanish-language newspapers, two Latino television programs, and several Latino and farm worker organizations.

Be realistic about where you believe you can get articles published or printed. If you're going to list *The New Yorker*, *Atlantic Monthly*, or even *Redbook*, you're going to have to indicate prior successful publication or some personal contact; otherwise you'll lose credibility.

If you don't want to commit to writing magazine articles or seeking reviews, perhaps you wouldn't mind sending flyers on your book to those on your personal mailing list. Many writers have now become adept with the graphics and art programs of computer software. If you've got the skills, offer to work with your publisher on developing a flyer and a pitch letter. If appropriate, offer to pursue direct-mail contact with suppliers of a retail item—cookware for a cookbook or garden equipment for a gardening book—with the expectation of establishing retail outlets for your book.

MEDIA APPEARANCES

Perhaps your book will sell well enough for your publisher to send you on a limited, nationwide promotional tour. For instance, the five coauthors of *Mothering Twins* were sent to a national twins convention by Fireside, the publishing imprint of Simon & Schuster. Whether or not a publicity tour is in the offing, include a sentence indicating your willingness (if you are) to "travel, speak, and promote anywhere in the country at the publisher's arrangement," or "to participate in any publisher's author's tour."

In addition to book signings and tours arranged by your publisher at the publisher's expense, this section allows you to offer media events or bookstore appearances by your own arrangement or with some publisher assistance. For instance, you could offer to arrange book signings locally or regionally with independent and chain bookstores, such as Waldenbooks, B. Dalton Bookseller, or others. You can offer to contact local or regional television and radio stations for talk and interview shows. Plan to contact newspapers about reviews and interviews. If you know someone or have made prior appearances on a station, name the show, station, and/or show host. The agent/editor is not going to believe that you can get yourself on Oprah, unless "About the Author" suggests it, or unless you can offer proof of a believable connection.

Giving a lecture or saying a few words to a club is different than being a professional speaker. Professional means that you get paid for being a speaker and that you know how to give a speech. Speaker's bureaus exist to help match organizations with proven professional speakers. Authors, of course, can make interesting speakers, but only if they are professionals in public speaking. If you qualify, state how you will use this skill.

PUBLICISTS

Publicists are marketing professionals whose job it is to secure publicity for your book. Like any consultants, they vary in skill, in fees, and in their connections. I have been told about fees that range from hundreds of dollars to thousands of dollars. Obviously, hiring a publicist can eat up your advance, when so much promotion can be done by you and your publisher.

List your intent to hire a publicist only if you anticipate selling your book to a mid- to large-size publisher or expect an advance large enough to sustain this cost. Certainly, if you foresee publication with a small, regional, or specialty publisher, your advance will be low—excluding extra money to hire a publicist and negating the need for one.

If you don't know a publicist to put down by name in your "About Promotion," then merely state your intention to hire a publicist from a portion of your advance monies.

The best way to find a publicist is by word of mouth. When the time comes, ask your agent or other published authors for names. Avoid making a commitment to the first one with whom you talk. Interview several and select the one whose plan, personality, and fees you find most agreeable.

An advantage to working with a publicist is that a good one knows how to approach major network talk shows. They have connections you can't easily make. Every book and every author is unique, and a good publicist will tailor a promotional plan to your needs.

Troubleshooting

Two considerations about promotion deserve special mention. They involve writers who:

- Prefer not to promote or are cash short; and
- Plan extensive promotion from independent resources.

PREFER NOT TO PROMOTE OR ARE CASH SHORT

If, for whatever reasons, you prefer not to promote your book, begin this section with a general statement indicating your willingness to cooperate with the publicity department. You can say yes or no later to specific requests not to your liking.

Even if you are unwilling to make public appearances, perhaps you would have no objections to offering your personal or professional mailing list to the publicity department. Perhaps you can offer to write letters requesting reviews or suggesting articles.

If you want nothing to do with promotion and your advance allows it, plan to hire a publicist. Although psychophysiologist George H. Green indicated willingness to promote his book in the usual ways, he and his coauthor, Carolyn Cotter, learned from a publicist that virtually all of their book's promotion could be handled with press releases, radio spots, and book reviews. They hired her. Carolyn is now working on her next book with a coauthor/expert who, as part of their working agreement, made the contingency that he not be required to promote the book.

Many writers tend to be cash short, time short, or both. The expectation for promoting your book involves at least some monies and time, and time translates into money.

If you anticipate being short of cash by the time your book enters production and is released, suggest ideas in your "About Promotion" that involve primarily time. Then begin to mentally prepare for, if not physically budget, a percentage of your work week—after you've finished writing your book—toward promotion. In the appendix of his bestseller, *The Self-Publishing Manual*, Dan Poynter, has a great month-by-month checklist of promotional ideas that can help any author. For the guerrilla marketer, a wonderful resource is John Kremer's *1001 Ways to Market Your Books*. Other helpful books are listed in this book's Resource Directory. Much promotion can be done with a small outlay of money—mostly for the cost of office supplies and postage.

One writer I met orchestrated the promotion of his self-published book entirely by appearances on radio talk shows. His expenses included postcards and postage for mailing his pitch to talk-show hosts across the country, and later for setting up an 800-line and credit-card billing for the orders that flooded in. His method of promotion became so successful that he eventually hired a telephone service with multiple 800-lines to handle the large influx of calls. This writer had the gift of gab. He had tallied 650 radio-talk shows, all secured at the cost of postcards and long-distance follow-up calls. He never left his house to promote his book.

If a radio-talk-show forum sounds like your bailiwick, offer to pursue this in your promotion section and read books on how to do it.

Don't make generous offers to promote your book in other regions or nationally at your own expense, if you can't do so. Transportation costs, food, and lodging can mount up, even for travel within your state. On the other hand, you may have friends or family in many locales who can offset lodging and food costs. Perhaps you're intending to make a recreational trip to another state anyway, or could. Offer what you can deliver.

PLAN EXTENSIVE PROMOTION FROM INDEPENDENT RESOURCES

Some writers have financial backing from corporations which, independent of the publisher, have their own marketing, sales, and publicity departments. Other writers possess the means and funds to hire a public relations firm. You may be in a position to buy a large number of your books for resale or giveaways. You may be able to buy advertising or obtain it through connections. You may know the "right" people with power and access to print and television media.

If you were a member of the editorial committee, how would you react to a writer with independent resources or backing? Such writer's ability to promote increases the likelihood of a higher advance or better book contract, for obvious reasons; they can absorb a publisher's promotion expenses, and to some degree, guarantee sales. If this describes your situation, make your "About Promotion" detailed. Also, make sure you broadcast your connections, financial resources, and influence in "About the Book" and "About the Author."

CHAPTER THIRTEEN

Last But Not Least: The Appendix

The Concept Statement
About the Book
About the Author
About the Market
About the Competition
Production Details
About Promotion
Table of Contents
Chapter Summaries
Sample Chapters
• **The Appendix**

Chapter Goal: To assemble exhibits that enhance your credibility and the importance and timeliness of your book.

"The Appendix" contains materials that supplement and "dress up" your proposal. It should deliver a positive first impression of your proposal. This may seem strange since "appendix" implies something at the end of more important information. However, like the prize in the Cracker Jack box, the appendix serves an important role that is both decorative and functional.

Definition and Purpose

"The Appendix" is a collection of publicity exhibits about you and your book's subject. Its purpose is to show off your past accomplishments in order to further persuade an agent/editor that you are qualified to write the book. Secondly, "The Appendix" provides ancillary support for the worthiness and timeliness of your book, as well as supports how you intend to sell it and your credentials. Its scope is limited only by your imagination.

Contents

"The Appendix" may contain an assortment of documents and exhibits. Here is a list and description of possibilities from which you may select.

DOCUMENTS

1. Published writing samples. These clips, photocopies of articles, ads, or anything else you've written and published, are among the most important documents. If you have many credits, or if the clips are for subjects unrelated to your book's subject, include a bibliography of your published works.

2. Published material about you. This might include newspaper articles about you, your hobby, or business. Have you been written up in a *Who's Who* or a trade biography? Photocopy your entry. Has someone else given you acknowledgment in his or her book? Include a copy in "The Appendix."

3. Published material about your book's subject. Remember that your proposal must answer the questions, "Why this book? Why now?" Photocopy recent newspaper articles or magazine features on your subject to show its popularity or timeliness.

4. Copies of promotional material about yourself or your business. This might include flyers about workshops, brochures, or advertisements related to your business and your book's subject.

5. Copies of award certificates or letters of commendation. Make sure they are related to your book or your writing.

6. Copies of reviews of your prior books, artistic creations, or technical inventions not necessarily related to this book.

7. A complete resume. While a resume is inappropriate in "About the Author," you may include one in "The Appendix." Do so only if you have had to omit significant or substantial background in your author section.

8. A written summary of television, radio, and movie coverage of your subject, citing programs or movie names and dates, only if this seems relevant to your book.

EXHIBITS

1. Sample illustrations, cartoons, photographs, charts, and graphs. Send copies or photocopies, never originals. Label everything.
2. Videotapes. You may send a videotape of yourself speaking in a television interview, giving a lecture on your book's subject, or promoting yourself and your subject commercially. Cliché that it is, a picture *is* worth a thousand words.
3. Audio tapes. If you have a clear audio tape of a radio interview, or an audio tape as part of your promotional material, or even one recording of a lecture you've given, label and send it—but only if it is a flattering and relevant representation of you and the book.
4. Author photograph. While it may be useful for promotion, the photo is at first unimportant, although it's a common addition to most proposals. If it's a mug shot, make sure its professional quality, either black-and-white or color. A high-quality laser color copy is sufficient. If you have good-quality photographs of yourself in an action related to your book, use them too. Avoid shots of you and Furface-the-Cat or of you and the kids on summer vacation. If your book is on kayaking and someone took a shot of you plunging into a class-six rapids on the Yangtze, that's a different story. Send it.

Presentation

Most agents package proposals in double-pocketed folders or as loose pages stacked in a manuscript box. An agent may place some of your appendix material so that it is the first thing an editor sees. Even if "The Appendix" is left at the end of the proposal after an editor has read through your manuscript, it offers a contrast both visually and stylistically to the proposal itself.

Presentation is important. Avoid the impression that your agent/editor is rifling through a musty shoebox collection of your past. Take odd-sized copies of articles, reviews, ads, or other printed documents and photocopy them onto 8 ½" x 11" paper. If you need to, make enlargements or reductions. Cut and paste and rearrange until you have visually appealing documents.

When a published article has appeared on page 38 of a magazine or in section F of your newspaper, cut it out and eliminate competing articles or advertisements. Consider placing this clip under the masthead of the magazine or newspaper, still providing the header that shows the date and page number where it originally appeared. This dresses up your articles, improves their presentation, and makes them easier to read.

When it comes to reproducing your flyers, workshop notices, or brochures, if the originals are blah, copy them onto colored paper—simply for the visual stimulation this provides. If your entire appendix material is on white paper, consider adding blank color papers as separators between different types of material. Think presentation as well as organization.

For photocopies of articles or features about your subject that include color photographs, make laser color copies for their visual appeal. This adds cost, especially if your agent requests ten copies of your proposal for marketing, but doing so makes the whole package more attractive. It is one of the "plus" values that is easy for you to achieve.

You know why you've included particular exhibits in "The Appendix" but will an agent/editor? Use a highlighter to circle what you want them to notice. Glue a caption over an article or feature to explain its relevance to you or to your subject. Make it easy for your reader. Add a cover sheet as page one of "The Appendix" with a table of contents, with or without page numbers.

Some writers go to even greater lengths to make an impression by sending t-shirts, baked goods, or other "promo hype." I don't recommend it. In answer to my question about whether he had received unusual items with proposals, one New York editor said, "I've received t-shirts, coffee mugs and bags of coffee beans, baseball cards, signed author photos, and other stuff. It doesn't influence me at all."

Problems With "The Appendix"

Rarely will a writer have too much material for "The Appendix." Include rather than exclude items, knowing that your agent can eliminate what he or she considers too much, or irrelevant. A greater problem exists for writers who have little or nothing for "The Appendix."

If you believe you have nothing to put in an appendix, double-check the possibilities listed above. Nearly everyone can do research and find something written about a book's subject in magazines or journals. However, let's suppose that you are writing original material, never before described in print.

Have you ever spoken on the topic? Could you speak or lecture and arrange for an audio or video tape? Can you generate some visuals—graphs or charts that translate your written ideas into some kind of display? If this isn't your forte, ask a teacher friend to help you (many teachers are geniuses at creating visual displays). Or, employ a copy or print shop that has a graphic artist who can help.

What Not to Include

Don't include any document or exhibit that would devalue you or trivialize your book's worthiness. For instance, you may remember my mention of the therapist whose appendix included photocopies of her articles published in *Nails* magazine. Articles on manicure or coiffure had nothing to do with the subject of her book and potentially reduced the presentation of herself as a professional in the field of mental health.

Also, eliminate rejection letters from other agents or publishers, even if their letterhead is embossed, and even if they had kind words to say about your writing. Rejection letters plant the thought of rejection. If your agent or editor asks where else you've sent your proposal, then you can supply an accounting of your rejections.

Evaluate carefully any letters of commendation or recommendation. If the person writing them is unknown or working for a local company, agency, or institution, the letter may convey a small-time image. Including them *may* make you seem provincial, not a quality considered charming— or marketable. Exclude documents of a controversial or politically incorrect nature, unless they relate directly to your book's subject. Perhaps you were one of the protesters a campus building featured by a newspaper. Put these clips away to share with your offspring.

Materials that would reveal your age, religion, sexual orientation, or racial group might not be relevant to your book, but they do reveal private information about you. Agents and editors are people first, and they too carry biases. Supply only information that is relevant to your book and will enhance its sale.

Last of all, if you have nothing for your appendix and choose not to create material, you haven't forfeited all chances for seeing your book published. This is, after all, the *appendix*, the postscript, to your proposal. If the rest of your proposal is well-written, fully developed, and professionally presented, you're going to get a sincere reading, with or without "The Appendix."

Now it's really time to celebrate; you have a complete, first draft of your proposal. "Put it to bed," meaning lay it aside. In the next chapter, you'll learn how to revise it from a fresh perspective.

CHAPTER FOURTEEN

Marketing Strategies: Queries and Responses, Agents and Editors

Chapter Goal: To write a compelling query and to develop a marketing strategy that leads to a request for your proposal.

Many years ago, I taught a series of mini-workshops covering everything from writing novels and magazine articles to proposals. A few weeks after the series, I received a call from an excited student.

"It works!" she proclaimed. "I kind of didn't believe it would, but I followed your instructions for writing a query letter for a book idea. I sent it out as a multiple submission to twenty editors, and guess what?"

"One wants it?" I guessed.

"No, seventeen want it," she told me. "And I haven't even started my proposal."

My student did one thing right; she started her marketing process with a query letter. As mentioned in chapter one, agents and editors prefer a query describing your book project and offering a proposal. In fact, her query yielded exactly what a writer hopes. What she didn't do according to Hoyle is have her proposal nearly finished and ready to send out in response. To her credit, she sacrificed all of her free time for the next two months and blitzed a proposal together.

Later, when you've written a proposal or two and know how long it takes you to write one, you might test the waters with a query letter, knowing that you have the know-how to bang out a proposal quickly.

> When you can follow up a request for your proposal with no more than two weeks delay, begin sending queries.

The Query Letter

On a basic level, a query letter for a book is a business letter asking an agent/editor if he or she is interested enough in your book idea to see a proposal. However, it is much more than a trial balloon. It is the first evidence of your writing. The query letter becomes a showcase of your writing; your command over organization, style, grammar, punctuation, and spelling. Because the marketplace is flooded with correspondence from writers seeking publication, the query letter is also your first sales pitch, your first foot in the door.

In a response letter to a student of mine, literary agent Denise Marcil reported that she receives an average of 100 query letters each week. She gives a generous yes to an average of 10.

By now, having written a rough draft of your proposal, you're an expert at writing sales' documents. After all, every section of your proposal is a sales pitch.

And, like every section of your proposal, the query letter has a lead, a body, and a conclusion. It may also have enclosures.

LEAD

You can craft an arresting lead by drawing from the list of possibilities offered in chapter eight, "About the Book." For instance, try a short anecdote or a startling statement, a statistic, or a comparison. You may be able to pirate your lead from "About the Book" or your concept statement and use it verbatim for your query. Here's a lead for a query letter written by the five authors of the book on twins:

> "Help!" is the first thought in the mind of the woman facing the frightening/exciting prospect of having twins. She wants to know firsthand what it's *really* like. Five mothers are filling a publication void by joining their stories in a book titled *Mothering Twins: A Labor of Love.*"

An equally acceptable query lead rejects the bells and whistles of a clever lead in favor of a clear, concise statement of purpose. A straightforward lead might start with the subject: "I am writing a book for writers on nonfiction book proposals," Or, it might start with author credentials: "I am an editor and writing teacher with fifteen years experience. I would like to supply a publishing void for a how-to book for writers on nonfiction book proposals."

BODY

In the body of your query letter, you should expand upon the subject of your book, the market for it, and its competition. Does this sound familiar? It should. You've done all of the research and writing to know precisely what makes your book better or different than others. You identified your strongest market and you researched the competition.

Because query letters are meant to be short—no more than two pages— you must address the subject, the market, and the competition in a few paragraphs. Some writers "lift" portions of their concept statements to supply the brevity and pizzazz to capture agent/editor attention.

Within the body, don't forget to rely upon specifics to focus your query on the need for your book. That's a mark of professionalism as a writer. Use specifics, such as quotes from a leading magazine or famous person, a statistic that provides evidence of your market, and authors and titles of one or two competitors with a few words about their shortcomings.

The five authors of *Mothering Twins* used specifics to successfully shape and polish their query to editors. I've picked the specifics out of their query letter to give you an idea of how they can be used.

Specifics	Its Purpose
An article on twins in *Newsweek Magazine*, Nov. 23, 1989, stated, "Sometimes, the best advice comes from twins and their parents who have been through it all. "	Supports their book's unique approach offering personal accounts from five mothers.
Other books on the market address the "how-to's" of parenting multiples... [ours] provid[es]...practical knowledge and validation for the feelings and work	Describes need that their book addresses and contrasts theirs with competition.
TWINS Magazine, circulation 40,000... 33,000 sets of twins born each year... 4.5 million twins and their families	Gives indication of size of market for the book.

A final paragraph or two in the body must supply author credentials, unless you opt for attaching a page of author biography. This is perfectly acceptable and a route I recommend if you have substantial qualifications for writing the book. Even if you attach a bio, write a line or two, or a small paragraph, in case the agent/editor doesn't want to take the time to read an enclosure.

When you select from your many credentials for use in the query, pick the strongest ones and those most relevant to the book. Review what you selected for "About the Author;" you may find lines or a paragraph you can simply copy. Pretend you are your own public-relations person and talk up your client.

CONCLUSION

Wrap up your query letter with a strong handshake. Offer to send your proposal, give thanks, and affirm your desire for a speedy response. Here is one generic close to a query that includes these three items:

> I would be happy to send you a proposal on _____
> _____ (your book's title). Thank you for your consider-
> ation. I look forward to hearing from you at your earliest conven-
> ience.

Sometimes, I've added a P.S. to a query. In a postscript, I am more personal, adding a comment or two regarding how I learned about this agent or editor, perhaps from reading about them in a directory or hearing good things about them from a friend. It is one way to acknowledge a human connection. It's also good sales. Here is a postscript written by one of my student's at the end of a query to Jean Naggar Literary Agency: "I have long heard wonderful things about your agency from writer, P. H., and especially liked what you had to say in Jeff Herman's *Insider's Guide* [to Book Editors, Publishers, and Literary Agents]."

If this student had a stronger connection to Jean Naggar— having met her at a writers' conference—I would have suggested mentioning that connection in a lead paragraph.

ENCLOSURES

If you plan to send anything with your query letter, then add "enc." below your letter signature and list your enclosures. You may enclose an author biography, as mentioned. I highly recommend including a table of contents of your proposed book and a photocopy or two of some article or feature relevant to your book or your author credentials. In other words, you don't want to load down the query package, but you do want to select what will make the best first impression.

After you've written your query letter, plan to rewrite it again and again. I know some writers who have spent as much as twenty hours on this one- or two-page document.

> Remember, your query and your enclosures have only one purpose: to gain a request to see your proposal.

They literally examined every word, every sentence, every paragraph. They played with order; they substituted one approach for another. They asked an eagle-eyed editor to help them proofread for mistakes. I'm a believer in the theory that you can't spend too much time on a query letter or have too many critics review it.

You won't get to impress an agent/editor with your proposal unless they say yes to your query. Nevertheless, you can only do what you can do. If you follow these instructions, your query letter will be good enough.

At a later date, you will probably come back to the query you sweated over for hours and decide it can be improved. If the agents or editors to whom you first sent it have rejected it, take the time to rewrite it before sending it out again. For example, I'm no longer satisfied with my query letter (the second one listed next in the sample queries), yet it met my specs when I wrote it many years ago. The fact that it yielded numerous requests for my proposal means that it served its only purpose: it got my foot in the door.

The point is, don't dash off a letter, like you might simple business correspondence. Instead, polish your query as if it were a contest entry with a prize of $20,000 to the winner, the average investment capital spent on a book by some publishing houses.

Two Sample Queries

The query letter in Sidebar 14-1 was written by psychologist Dr. Kathleen McGuire. It succeeded in attracting an agent request for her proposal and then representation. In contrast to most queries, Dr. McGuire's included her proposal—because she had talked with the agent prior to sending her work. Sadly, her proposed book did not sell, as I'll explain later in this chapter.

Sample: Query Letter

Dear _____:

I would like you to consider my book, *Moved To Tears: The Meaning and Joy in Learning To Cry*. I have enclosed a detailed proposal and sample chapters.

General Norman Schwarzkopf cried on national television when he spoke of the death of Desert Storm warriors. At that moment, the world turned. It became possible for anyone to cry.

Schwarzkopf concretized a change in the *zeitgeist* well under way: Oprah Winfrey, Bernie Siegel, John Bradshaw, and Robert Bly were already extremely popular advocates for tears. Since Schwartzkopf, articles on tears have appeared in *Glamour*, *Arthritis Today*, and *Mothering*, to name a few. Editorials in major news weeklies and syndicated newspaper columns argue the pros and cons of crying. The time has come for a book on how to cry.

Moved To Tears: The Meaning and Joy in Learning To Cry teaches crying as a learnable skill. It shows that tears reduce stress, increase intimacy, and allow access to positive emotions as well as to pain. Most importantly, it explains the meaning of tears: tears alert us to profound personal values. By showing what matters, they can lead to decisions that bring meaning into life.

Moved to Tears teaches readers to cry, then uses Eugene Gendlin's focusing technique to explore the meaning of tears. Gendlin's *Focusing* (Bantam, 1981) has been constantly reprinted and has been translated into eight languages. The Focusing Institute in Chicago trains hundreds of people each year and recently received a grant of $300,000 to broaden its work.

I trained personally with Dr. Gendlin at the University of Chicago, where I received a Ph.D. in Clinical Psychology in 1975. Dr. Gendlin remains a colleague and will write the forward for *Moved To Tears*.

I am a licensed psychologist, specializing in grief and Inner Child work, as well as in peer self-help. I have led workshops in the United States and Europe and have sold over one thousand copies of my self-help manual, *Building Supportive Community: Mutual*

Self-Help Through Peer Counseling. I have written for professional and popular publications.

Moved to Tears will have approximately 100,000 words. I could deliver the book eighteen months after first advance.

There is presently no competition for *Moved To Tears*. Self-help books talk about how to have feelings but do not teach how to cry. I hope we can work together to bring *Moved To Tears* to a large and eager audience.

Sincerely,
Kathleen N. McGuire, Ph.D.

Because short is sweet in the land of query letters, if you can reduce yours to one page, all the better. That was my goal when I first marketed this book. Again, the query (Sidebar 14-2) was a success, measured by the fact that it drew requests from editors of major publishing houses.

Marketing Strategies

Once you've finished drafting and polishing your query letter, you face five tasks before sending it. You must:

- Choose between agents and editors;
- Decide whether to market to agents and editors simultaneously;
- Find an agent or editor;
- Evaluate agent/editor qualifications; and
- Develop a marketing strategy.

CHOOSE BETWEEN AGENTS AND EDITORS

Every book demands a different marketing strategy, and every writer has a unique set of values and preferences. Agents sell proposals to editors, and editors pitch proposals to publishing committees. Some writers look at this chain of sales and decide they will be one step ahead if they market directly to editors of publishing houses. This may or may not be to a writer's advantage. Others decide to play both hands and market to agents and editors simultaneously. Sidebar 14-3 shows some differences between marketing to an agent and marketing to an editor.

With the exception of the special cases I will discuss at the end of the

Sample: Query Letter

Dear (Editor's Name):

Whenever I hear the words, "I've spent five years researching and writing my book, would you take a look at it and help me find a publisher?" I am torn between admiration and pathos. I admire anyone who actually writes a book. I am happy to tell that person that 85 percent of the 50,000 books published each year are nonfiction, and that most of that group has been written by first-time authors. On the other hand, as an editor and literary consultant, I suffer by having to tell aspiring authors, "Agents and editors don't want to read a finished book. They want a book proposal, which you'll have to learn how to write."

Since 1988, I've been a freelance writing instructor at Lane Community College in Eugene, Oregon. I teach classes on how to write book proposals in a report style, which I learned from literary agent Natasha Kern, rather than in a letter style. Although I have been using and recommending existing books on proposals, all fall short. They were written "agent-down" rather than "writer-up." These books fail to provide step-by-step instruction and omit analysis of sample proposals by *first-time* authors.

Because of these deficiencies, I began writing how-to material and collecting sample proposals, which I would now like to market as a book, *Nonfiction Book Proposals for First-time Authors* [my working title]. My proposal, by the way, won first place in a contest for proposals sponsored by The National Writers Club. May I send you my proposal? To give you an overview of the work, I have enclosed the table of contents. I look forward to hearing from you soon.

Sincerely,
Elizabeth Lyon

enc: table of contents

chapter, I recommend seeking an agent to help you market your proposal if your market is mid-sized or large. Agents do much more for writers than find publishers and finagle higher advances. They are publishing experts. As literary agent Natasha Kern expressed in an article for *Writer's Northwest*

Handbook (Fifth Edition):

> Agenting requires understanding sales and marketing (they are not the same thing); literary law; editing; publishing business practices; industry standards; requirements and protocols; publicity and promotion; counseling and career development; international and film rights markets; arbitration and a myriad of other things including the rapidly burgeoning opportunities in high-tech publishing.

DECIDE WHETHER TO MARKET TO AGENTS AND EDITORS SIMULTANEOUSLY

If your book is aimed at a market large enough to warrant agent representation, there's no reason not to query agents and editors at the same time. Although I recommend pursuing any referrals or requests—agent or editor—first, if you're working from unfamiliar names in directories, then market to both groups. By querying editors at publishing houses, you could eliminate the long passages of time while waiting to find an agent who in turn will approach editors where you must wait again. If you find an interested publisher, you'll also have no trouble finding an agent. By taking over marketing and finding a buyer, you'll be attractive indeed to an agent. You will even be in a position to interview agents and choose your favorite.

Why get an agent if you've already found a publisher? You may feel comfortable working directly with your editor. In the Resource Directory, I've listed some books that offer guidance for negotiating your own contract. However, agents are contract experts, and for all of the reasons mentioned previously, have many more functions that may be helpful in the life of a writer.

FIND AN AGENT OR EDITOR

Several matchmaking methods exist for connecting writers with agents and editors. Successful "marriages" have blossomed from each one. The primary goal is to find one that works for you.

You may find an agent/editor through:

- Face-to-face contact;
- Word-of-mouth recommendations; and
- Directories or listings.

Pros and Cons of Marketing to Agents and Editors

Advantages With Agents

1. Ninty percent of all books published have been agent submitted. With an editor, you may get a lower priority reading. Most large publishers refuse unagented material.

2. Agents know which houses and editors are buying. Your work could get lost or rejected by the "wrong" editor.

3. Agents can reach editors with more clout. You may have to work up through readers to a senior editor.

4. Agents can make multiple submissions and arrange auctions. Generally, you may submit only one proposal at a time to editors.

5. Agents work for you; they usually negotiate for more money, subsidiary rights, and protection clauses.

6. Editors work for publishers. They may use a poorer contract for writers without agents.

7. An agent can act as a buffer between an editor and writers. Agents absorb rejection and act as mediators on your behalf. You're blessed or stuck with dealing with your editor, and they've got the power.

8. Agents help sculpt your career. They can market future works to other publishers. Editors work to save money. Their first concern is the bottom line, not you.

9. Agents receive letters of explanation for rejected materials. Writers more often get form rejections.

10. Because editors have long-term relationships with agents, they respond more quickly to agent submissions than to those sent by writers.

11. Editors come and go; an agent works for the long-haul.

12. Through publishers, monies from the sale of subsidiary sales are applied against the advance. Agents usually reserve many subsidiary rights, so the writer can receive those monies before the advance is earned out.

Advantages With Editors

1. You receive all advance monies and royalties as specified in your contract. Agents claim 15 percent commissions on all monies you receive.

2. Editors read for free. Some agents charge reading fees.

3. You pay for marketing that your agent does on your behalf. After you have a contract, publishers pay for any mailings on your behalf.

4. You reach "The Source" directly and enjoy a relationship uncomplicated by a person in the middle.

5. Marketing time is on your side. You are active, not passive. Months or years may go by waiting for an inefficient agent to market or respond to you.

6. With one book to market, your research can find the right publisher. Agents have favorite editors and houses. If your book doesn't fit these, it may never be sent to the right house or editor.

7. You receive more money dealing directly with an editor. On a first book, an agent may not secure a better contract or get you more money, yet you pay their 15 percent commission forever.

8. Time and effort to find an editor shortcuts the process. It's easy to find an agent after you've got a publisher.

9. You spend time and effort just to find an agent. You must still wait while they market to publishers.

10. Agents often don't handle specialized books, or books to small or regional houses.

Face-to-face Contact

In an ideal universe, you would meet face to face with one hundred agents and editors. Then you would select each other based upon personal chemistry, shared goals, and the merits of your proposal. For most writers, it is not possible to ring up one, much less 100 agents or editors, to suggest that you "do lunch." Even if you live in the same city with a literary agent, don't expect a warm response to your invitation to get together. Agents don't have the time and, to tell the truth, with a 99 percent rejection rate, it would be unprofitable for them to meet you. As a result, agents and editors prefer query letters.

Regardless, a great way to gather first impressions and a sense of relationship is to go to writer's conferences where agents and editors attend. These publishing professionals not only turn out because it is good public relations for their firms, they attend in order to meet writers. They really are talent scouts, hoping to meet the next Dr. John Gray (*Men Are From Mars Women Are From Venus*) or Elizabeth Marshall Thomas (*The Hidden Life of Dogs*), or Thomas Moore (*Soul Mates*).

In their May issue, *Writer's Digest Magazine* publishes a list of some of the hundreds of writer's conferences that take place each year. You can also learn what conferences take place in your region by contacting any local arts association, local or regional chapters of writers' organizations, and through directories stocked by most libraries (See Resource Directory). Ask your local reference librarian to track down conferences that take place near you. The information may even be accessible on-line.

The benefit of face-to-face meetings with agents or editors is that you can get a lot accomplished instantly. While both of you are recording your impressions of each other as people, you'll be discussing your book project. Best of all, you'll get an on-the-spot yes or no to your book idea, without having to wait weeks or months for your proposal to reach the top of someone's desk.

Word-of-mouth Recommendations

Word-of-mouth remains the best sales tool in existence. Everyone in business builds a reputation. You can get name referrals, especially for agents but also for editors, by asking anyone with a connection to the publishing industry. Go to book signings and presentations and talk with authors. Call or meet with your friendly manager of Barnes and Noble or one of your area's independent bookstores. If you get an editor interested in your book, ask him or her for referrals to trustworthy agents. Talk with freelance editors and writing teachers, or with a book-review editor at your newspaper. Call editors or publishing consultants listed in your yellow pages. Pretty soon, you'll hear a repetition of names or receive a resounding recommendation.

> Every writer I know who has gone to a conference and met with agents or editors has returned with at least one request to send material.

Directories or Listings

Even if you live in an igloo hundreds of miles above the Arctic Circle, you can find an agent or editor by letting "your fingers do the walking." Instead of the telephone book (unless you live in New York where some hundred agents are listed), consult the directories shown in Sidebar 14-4.

EVALUATE AGENT/EDITOR QUALIFICATIONS

Much more difficult than finding names of agents and editors is evaluating whether or not the agent/editor is qualified and the right match for your project. Agents and editors, like any other professionals, come in three categories: great at what they do, good at what they do, and not so good.

Literary Agents

A literary agent may be great for one author and so-so for another. Just like trying to find a good dance partner, you can't tell about someone until you get out on the floor.

Directories will help you make an initial judgment. For instance, you can find out how long an agent has been in business and whether or not she belongs to the AAR which, as a membership requirement, demands agreement to a code of ethics and demonstration of success. Look closely at the types of books an agent prefers, titles of recent sales, and the percentage of nonfiction represented.

While the directories often list recent sales by title and publisher, you can write to an agent and request a client list or a list of recent sales. (Do enclose an SASE.) Postpone this step, however, until an agent has

Sidebar 14-4
Key Agent and Editor Directories

- *The Literary Market Place*: Lists several hundred agent and editor names, addresses, and preferences.

- *Literary Agents of North America*: Lists and describes the most agents, about 1000, including Canadian agents.

- *Guide to Literary Agents*, a paperback directory you can purchase from Writers Digest Books: Lists about 400agents, their basic credentials, what they are looking for, and divides them into those who charge a reading fee and those who don't. It also identifies those agents who represent children's works.

- *Insider's Guide to Book Editors, Publishers, and Literary Agents* by Jeff Herman (Prima Publishing): The only guide that gives in-house editor names and their specialties. It also offers the most detailed description of any guide, but only of about 80 agents.

- The Association of Author's Representatives (AAR), the only professional organization for literary agents: Offers a members' list and a code of ethics, if you will send a legal-sized, self-addressed, stamped envelope (SASE) with two first-class stamps

continued

accepted your proposal. To be thorough, contact authors who are listed as clients. Check recent sales and determine the size, variety, and location of publishers. Are they large houses or obscure small ones? Do you see a predominance of sales to the same publishers, implying agent familiarity with only a few favorites?

While no one charges to read query letters, a growing number of agents charge a fee ranging from $25 to $75 to read and evaluate proposals. While this is strictly a processing fee, a minimal payment for the time and effort on the agent's part, it is not an editing fee. Given the thousands of queries and manuscripts, many agents employ clerks and readers. Any mention of "reading fees" above a reasonable and typical amount—$25 to $75—should raise a red flag. If a fee-charging agent rejects your work, you will usually receive a letter explaining why. De-

and $5 in check or money order to: AAR, 10 Astor Place, Third Floor, N.Y., N.Y. 10003.

- *Writer's Market* and *Children's Writer's and Illustrator's Market*: Lists and describes over 800 publishers, their needs, and the editors to whom you should address your query.

- *Writer's Handbook*, published by The Writer, Inc.: Lists and describes publishers and offers about 200 agent listings, though the description for each is Spartan.

- *The Christian Writer's Market*: Gives names and addresses of publishers specializing in the religious and inspirational market (Sally E. Stuart, Joy Publishing).

- *How to Get Your Teaching Ideas Published: A Writer's Guide to Educational Publishing*, (Walker & Co.).

- *Writing for the Educational Market* by Barbara Gregorich: A complete resource book for writing and publishing for many educational applications.

- *Writing for the Ethnic Markets* by Meera Lester: Provides names and descriptions of publishers who seek books targeted to ethnic audiences or with multicultural emphasis (Writer's Connection).

spite the fact that one-third of all agents now charge reading fees, many agents, as well as editors and publishers, believe it is wrong for agents to charge any fee for reading proposals they have requested.

"Editorial fees" introduce a greater dilemma. This is a fee charged to edit a work, not to sell it. Since most manuscripts are rejected by agents, one has to question whether an agent is making money from editorial services rather than from selling works. In the case of editorial services—ranging from several hundred to several thousand dollars—literary agents risk a conflict of interest. Writers will naturally assume that a revision according to the suggestions of one of these editor-type agents will open the door for representation of their books. It's the proverbial carrot on the stick. Although professional editing may be the best thing that happens to your book and your career, be wary about mixing editing with agenting in one person or agency. To avoid this conflict of interest, many agents maintain lists of professional editors to offer interested writers.

Although many of these facts can be researched before you commit to an agent, you should reserve some crucial questions of qualifications and compatibility until you've been accepted. Sometimes writers feel so relieved to have found an agent who likes their work and wants to represent them that they fail to ask other important questions that could make the difference in a good partnership. I'll introduce these questions later in the section on "Interpreting Responses."

Editors

It's much easier to get information about the performance of agents than of editors. The marketing directories give editor names and titles, and some offer an editor's specialty, but I haven't heard of a directory that spells out how long an editor has been in the business, or held a position, or for how many titles he or she has mentored authors from acquisition to publication. The problem of evaluating an editor's skill is complicated by the revolving door changes in personnel in most houses. An editor who acquires your book may not be employed with your publisher when it is published.

Your best hope of getting some impressions about editors is to meet them at writer's conferences and to track them through ardent reading of the trade journal for the industry, *Publishers Weekly*. A reference librarian can use computers to find every time an editor—or agent's—name has appeared in print. One particular technique for finding a "hungry" editor—or evaluating one—is to read the columns in *Publishers Weekly* called "People" and "Rights." You'll pick up the rumors and reports of who has moved where or sold what to whom. Here's where agents can also help. Good agents listen to the talking drums of the Big Apple. They hear stories and add their personal experience with editors to the rumors. If you work with an agent, he or she is your best barometer for measuring an editor's skill and compatibility with your project; conversely, an astute editor can steer you toward a qualified agent.

DEVELOP A MARKETING STRATEGY

Let's suppose you've culled through directories, received some word-of-mouth recommendations, and even met some agents or editors at a workshop. From this, you have identified several dozen agents or editors to whom your project could be sent. What's next? What will further your goals?

First, you must be sensitive to the issue of "simultaneous submissions." This refers to mailing a submission, meaning query or proposal, to more than one agent or editor at a time. Simultaneous submissions contrast with "exclusive submissions," in which the writer is expected to submit to the one agent/editor and wait for a response before marketing to anyone else.

Policies differ widely from one agency and publisher to another. Some agents make their preferences known in the agent directories. The best way to be clear about an agent or editors "rules," is to ask what the policy is in your query letter. Everyone in the industry recognizes

> Follow agent/editor instructions with regards to simultaneous submissions.

the insufferable passage of time while manuscripts are being processed. Many editors and agents find nothing wrong with writers submitting simultaneously, *as long as they are so informed*.

A strategy that puts you in control of the waiting process with an agent or editor who requests an exclusive is to inform the agent or editor that you will allow him or her six or eight weeks, after which, you'll begin to market it elsewhere.

From an agent or editor's point of view, instructions to you about what to submit and how constitute a kind of test. Northwest agent Natasha Kern said that if a writer won't follow her agency's instructions, it makes her wonder if she would have problems with communication later on. When a writer doesn't send in what an agent or editor requests, it plants an image of unreliability. On the other hand, writers are so used to kowtowing to agents and editors, they may have forgotten that communication is a two-way street, and they may make requests as well.

In the past, I've recommended to writers that they send a query or requested proposal exclusively to agents or editors they've met or been personally referred to. However, exclusive submissions can put you in the uncompromising position of no choice. If that agent or editor accepts your manuscript, do you then say "No, I want to shop around."? In the end, a writer's strongest position is the simultaneous submission.

Send simultaneous queries to as many agents and editors as you wish. Or send your query to one or the other. I suggest mailing in batches of ten. Although you could theoretically mail queries to all 800 agents in North America simultaneously and be done with marketing, this might hinder your chances of success more than help. Ten queries allow you to test the market and receive feedback. You'll find out whether your query will yield multiple requests for your proposal, form rejections, or rejections with reasons that could help you adapt your approach for the next batch.

The late Gaines Smith—a writer and editor to whom this book is dedicated—introduced me to the idea of staggered submissions. He noticed in directories that some agents and editors stated they responded to queries within six weeks. Others listed four weeks or two weeks or one week. He staggered the mailing of his queries in order to receive all responses back at the same time—theoretically, giving him maximum choice and allowing for the least amount of lag time between an agent request for his manuscript and mailing it.

> While non-fee-charging agents may receive more inquiries, a fee does not insure greater competency or a higher chance of acceptance.

Reading fees may also factor into your decision about who to query. Although no one charges to read a query, you may prefer querying agents who do not charge a fee to read your proposal. Of course, editors of publishing houses never charge reading fees.

If you have a referral to a fee-charging (if reasonable) agent or a request for your manuscript from one, send it to this agent first, fee or no fee, because recommendations and requests are golden. Any connection should receive a higher marketing priority than a name from a directory.

While marketing your book, first with a query and then with your proposal, only one taboo exists: Never query an agent or editor over the phone. When asked, agents and editors universally expressed a loathing of phone interruptions from writers wanting to pitch their ideas. *Send a query.*

That said, here's the inevitable exception: You may call a publisher in order to get the appropriate editor name. Occasionally this will put you in touch with a senior editor in charge of your book's subject, instead of with a secretary. Be prepared to describe your project. The editor may

> Phone queries are almost universally inappropriate.

invite you to submit your proposal. If so, you've just upgraded your submission from unsolicited to solicited. Let me reiterate, never—almost never—call an agent or editor.

Interpreting Responses From Query Letters

You can expect one of three responses to your query letters.

- A form rejection letter;
- A personalized rejection letter; or
- A go-ahead.

A FORM REJECTION LETTER

No doubt, form rejections are the curse of the entire publishing industry. Editors and agents don't enjoy sending them, and writers hate receiving them. Even a small publisher can easily spend ten hours per week saying no to unsolicited submissions and queries with SASEs. That's more than most can afford. But every query, no matter how tersely rejected, is first considered seriously. A competent editor is always hoping to find that one in a hundred. But most are not even targeted to the right publisher. That's one of the problems for which this book is a solution.

Most active agents receive 3000 to 5000 queries each year. If you were a one-person agency, perhaps with some clerical help, how would you respond to 50 to 100 queries each week when only half a dozen or fewer sounded interesting?

Take a form rejection at face value with nothing more intended. A refusal from one agent/editor may be a blessing to try another, better-suited one. A refusal from a publisher might signal a need on your part to make sure you're sending out to appropriate publishers for your subject and approach.

A PERSONALIZED REJECTION LETTER

If I can save you a beginner's error in judgment, don't take the rejection in a personalized rejection letter and fail to recognize the encouragement. Agents and editors don't write personal letters or notes out of the blue. Pay close attention. If an agent or editor goes to the trouble to explain why your query was rejected, you may be able to make adjustments, rewrite, and then resubmit to the same agent or editor. Your problem could be as simple as inexperience in crafting a good query. The agent/editor might feel unsure of your market; you can clarify or expand it by changing your slant. The agent/editor might feel uncertain you have adequate qualifications; you can send an expanded author biography and clips of articles about yourself or your subject.

You may get rejected a second time, but you will have earned respect as a writer willing to write and rewrite. You've actually begun a relationship. On the other hand, you may get accepted the second time. Your rewritten query may lead to a request for your proposal. Bull's-eye! In this case, the initial rejection has been transformed into an acceptance.

Although every agent and editor holds individual perceptions, biases, and taste, any comment by one of these professionals is worth serious consideration. You may be tempted to discard the reason for rejection, but more likely, you'll find some kernel of criticism that will help you adjust your approach.

A GO-AHEAD

Savor the exciting moment when an agent or editor says, "Yes!" You may even receive a phone call to your query, especially if the editor or agent is excited about your project and wants the kind of impressions that can only come from some kind of personal contact. They may call in order to gain assurance that someone else hasn't beaten them to the acquisition. It's great to be sought after. Stay on your toes, however. If the agent or editor asks you for an exclusive submission or any other kind of terms, be ready to express your delight in a request for your proposal, but keep your options open. You could suggest that you've already promised to let another agent or editor read the proposal, or you could certainly suggest a quick turnaround, say, four weeks.

If you have the opportunity of such a phone response, gather your wits. This is an appropriate time to ask further questions about your prospective agent or editor. Some of these questions are offered later in this chapter.

Based on a phone acceptance or a letter of acceptance, do not send your proposal prematurely. You have a window of two weeks or so in which to finish polishing and packaging your proposal. Use this time to make final rewrites. Two weeks is nothing in this industry of hurry-up-and-wait, at least not at this stage.

When you get that yes, it's time to polish, package, and send your proposal.

CHAPTER FIFTEEN

The Perfect Proposal: From Final Edit to Contract Offer

Chapter Goal: To polish your proposal and secure agent representation and editorial acceptance.

Polishing Your Proposal

While your query letters are zipping through the mails to their destinations, turn your full attention to revising, polishing, and packaging your proposal. You must edit your proposal at least three times for three different purposes: for content, for copy mistakes, and for format.

CONTENT EDIT

Playing the part of an editor, look at your proposal objectively for three content-related problems:

> Read your proposal aloud into the bright light of an early morning while assuming an objective attitude.

1. A good title;
2. Correct organization; and
3. Clear definition and purpose.

A Good Title

Although you've had a working title throughout the creation of the proposal, reexamine the title now. How well will it serve as a selling hook? Two guidelines may help.

- Market tests show that book purchasers respond most favorably to titles that are five words or less.
- Choose a descriptive title over a clever title in a New York minute. (*Cheapskate Decorating* is both!)

You can follow these guidelines, but use your subtitle to modify or better explain your book, especially if your main title is literary or poetic. For example, *We'll Remember in November: Molly Yard's Gift to Women's Rights*. Remember, too, your first customer is an agent/editor.

Correct Organization

One of the most important aspects of a content edit is to diagnose how clearly, logically, and appropriately you have organized each section. Confusing structure shows up as the most common "disease" in the proposals I "treat." For a high-energy manuscript, repair sections, paragraphs, sentences, and words that are out-of-order. Check each section against your outline and review the instructions in this book for each section.

Clear Definition and Purpose

Another goal of content editing is to ensure that each section of your proposal accomplishes its intended purpose. Review the statements of chapter goals in this book and those sections marked "definition and purpose."

COPY EDIT

Copy editing is like giving your manuscript a face lift. It refers to corrections of grammar, spelling, and punctuation. You've probably become so accustomed to your work that you may not even see those unsightly blemishes. Seek outside help for editing. It's a manifestation of Murphy's Law that once you send off your proposal, you'll look over your copy and find a typo—usually on page one.

Some of the most effective editing involves tightening, which means revising nearly every sentence, every paragraph, and every page. Clarify muddy thoughts and you'll find extra words to delete. Shorten a work and it becomes better.

FORMAT EDIT

Although many writers know about content and copy editing, proposals are specialized documents that also require editing for format. Two aspects of format that you must check are:

- Order of the proposal parts; and
- Graphic consistency.

Order of the Proposal Parts

Because this book has led you through the construction of a proposal in the order that is most helpful to writing it, you must now reorganize the sections for consideration by an agent or editor. A complete list of proposal parts in standard order is:

Title Page
The Concept Statement *
Proposal Table of Contents *
About the Book
About the Author *
About the Market *
About the Competition *
Production Details *
About Promotion *
Table of Contents
Chapter Summaries
Sample Chapters
The Appendix

Asterisk refers to sections that may be moved around to order by importance or for marketing reasons.

In earlier chapters, you learned about all the essential sections of the proposal. Now is the time to draft a title page and proposal table of contents, not to be confused with the table of contents for your book.

Title Page

You may use a larger-sized print to dress up your title. Use caps or bold or both. Don't use an underlined title, even though that is the grammatically correct way to show manuscript italics for a book title. This is a sales tool, not an English term paper. You can take certain liberties to enhance your product.

Sidebar 15-1
Title Page

[start one-third to one-half down]

THE BEST BOOK EVER
by
Jane E. Doe

Jane Doe
1 Main, Town 00000
503-555-5555

Proposal Table of Contents

The proposal table of contents looks like any other table of contents. Even so, think appearances, not just content. Line up indents, spaces, and periods to create a subtle but powerful graphic feeling of order and beauty. Seriously. For example:

GRAPHIC CONSISTENCY

In your format edit, check for the following items:

1. Consistent labeling;
2. Consistent font, size, and emphasis;
3. Consistent space and overall format.

Consistent Labeling

Throughout this book, I have used the same name for each of the proposal parts. The industry has no standard template for proposal design; nor is there one set of titles for each of the parts. One of my hopes is that this book will introduce a guideline for proposals that could serve as a prototype for an industry standard.

Regardless, no two books or authors are the same. The proposal must be flexible enough to accommodate individuality and creativity, yet it must remain clear to the reader. Where you feel an alteration in heading would better serve your subject or personality, know that you can make a change without breaking some rule.

Inconsistent section headings are as distracting as loud commercials during a favorite television movie. Because headings emphasize important divisions within your text and formulate "meaning bytes" (my term), it's important to think about their construction.

Check your headings according to the following guidelines:

- Make them brief, half a line or less;
- Use parallel syntax for same-level headings;
- Avoid using a long series of nouns or adjectives; and
- Eliminate double meanings and confusing terms.

Consistent Font, Size, and Emphasis

I owe my friend Stew Meyers, a technical editor, a debt of gratitude. He first brought to my attention "little" details that I had previously ignored. Technical writers like Stew are light years ahead in making written material accessible to readers. Stew pointed out to me that one level of accessibility (as well as aesthetics) is checking all headings to make sure they are consistent throughout an entire document.

> Clarity and consistency in format increases clarity of content.

Headings increase reader accessibility by their content and by the way they break up text visually. Make sure you use the same font, size, and emphasis for the headings at each level across all proposal sections. By level, I mean the heading that would correspond to the large Roman numerals I, II, III in an outline, then the A, B, C level, and then the 1, 2, 3 and so forth. If you look back over the headings in this book, you'll see consistency in headings by font, size, and emphasis for each level or hierarchy of information.

In this age of increasingly sophisticated software and printers, many writers have the capacity to create whatever size of type they choose. Do not use what was formerly called elite, or 12 characters to the inch.

If you are unsure about your type size, get out a ruler and count! You can depart from standard size, but only if you go slightly larger. You may also vary the font, but always choose for easy readability.

Size and emphasis (bold, uppercase, underline, etc.) correspond to levels of organization (hierarchy) and they mean easier access to your material by your readers. The following guidelines may help you make those decisions about these "little" details:

> The standard type size is still 10 characters per inch, no smaller, and the standard type font is Courier.

- Indentation shows more importance than non-indentation;
- Larger type shows more importance than smaller type;
- Upper case shows more importance than lower case, though studies show that upper case is slower to read;
- Bold shows more importance than non-bold;
- Bold and upper case show more importance than either alone; and
- Italics and underlining show more importance than using neither; however, both are considered harder to read.

Consistent Space and Overall Format

While you are checking your headings, also check your spacing. Make sure your right margin is *un*justified. Drop down the same amount of space from the top of each page to begin typing. Use the same spacing between text and the headings that follow and also between headings and the text that follows, between items on a list, and between lists and text. This may seem like going to extraordinary measures. Consistent format, including use of space, creates a subtle but powerful impact of order and professionalism. Released from the confusion of inconsistency, the agent/editor can focus on the content of your proposal.

Some agents/editors prefer double-spacing throughout, including sample chapters. Others accept single-spacing (with spaces left between paragraphs), as long as the sample chapters are double-spaced. I like to use lots of graphics in creating organizational units, both for visual relief and for reader stimulation.

> Consider overusing space rather than underusing it, since agents and editors spend most of their time looking at the printed page.

They simply don't look as good with double-spacing as with single-spacing. As a result, I prefer to use single-spacing for my proposal, making ample use of spaces between paragraphs and other visual effects. If you use many indented and bulleted lists, single-space your proposal. If you use mostly unbroken blocks of text, double-space your proposal. For clarity's sake, always double-space sample chapters.

Be generous with your margins. While professional specifications demand a minimum of a one-inch margin, studies show that readers prefer a print density of 40 percent. That means a page that shows only 40 percent print on it.

Use a 1" to 1.25" margin for all sides. It's standard to drop down six line spaces (or half an inch) before you begin your header—your name, title, and page number. However, you could drop another 0.75" to 1" in line space *after* the header.

Page numbering in your proposal should, by the way, be consecutive from your concept statement through to the last page of your last sample chapter.

If you'd rather be writing your book than editing for format, hire a perfectionist to do it for you.

Packaging Your Proposal

If you've gotten this far, you could send in your proposal simply typed with no special effects and you'd have a more professional presentation than most. But why stop here. Imagine your proposal as a shop filled with treasures. Agents and editors have never been inside this store before. Their first impressions begin with the display window. What's there should draw them inside.

Depending upon the proposal, the display window might be something from the appendix, such as your photo, a color photocopy of an article, or perhaps a clearly labeled video tape. Or, the display window might be an attractive title page on one side of a folder and the first page of the sample chapters on the other side, all with clear dark print on white paper. Arrange your material in the way that makes the best first impression.

Depending upon the length of your proposal and the additional bulk provided by material in your appendix, you may need to package your proposal in a standard manuscript box. These are available at most office-supply stores. If you do have a large proposal, stack it in the box in the following top-to-bottom order:

- Self-addressed, stamped envelope (SASE) for a reply and return postage for the manuscript;
- Cover letter; and
- The proposal.

In some cases, you may want to put your photograph or some impressive bit of publicity about yourself or your book after the cover letter.

If your proposal does not require a manuscript box, then use a simple, double-pocket folder. Two typical ways of packaging the proposal: 1) the main proposal and appendix material on one side and the sample chapters on the other side, or 2) the main proposal and sample chapters on one side and the appendix on the other. Either way, lay your cover letter on top of the right pocket, to be seen and read first. Put your SASE (with the correct postage for the return of the manuscript) under the cover letter.

Interpreting Responses to Your Proposal

While a go-ahead response to your query represents a foot in the door, the real test comes with reaction to your proposal. If you've secured agent representation, you'll receive editorial committee response too.

As with responses to your query, you can expect to receive one of three types of responses to your proposal:

- A personalized rejection;
- A qualified acceptance; or
- An enthusiastic acceptance.

A PERSONALIZED REJECTION

When an agent/editor has requested your proposal based upon a query and spent the time to read it, you're unlikely to get a form rejection. Explaining why the proposal was rejected is an understood courtesy. After all, you've probably granted this person an exclusive submission.

The explanation may be brief: "sales potential too small," "not quite right for our list," "the proposal was strong but the sample chapters disappointed," or "seems written for an academic audience." Rarely can you reinterest an agent/editor by attempting to improve your proposal based on these comments. Your best strategy is to accept the rejection and try elsewhere.

If an agent or editor tells you that your book's sales potential is too small or its market too specialized or competitive, you may have misjudged your book's potential. Perhaps you sent your query to the wrong type or size of publisher, or to an agent when you don't need one.

A QUALIFIED ACCEPTANCE

An agent/editor may ask you to rewrite or rethink some aspect of your book before he or she offers you representation or a contract. This kind of acceptance offers encouragement but no guarantee against subsequent rejection. However, you should be excited. You're close. Read the criticism and address the problems, then resubmit.

> Every agent is part editor, and every editor edits! Expect to revise your proposal.

AN ENTHUSIASTIC ACCEPTANCE

Whether you get this response to a first reading of your proposal or to a subsequent one, bask in the moments, or if you can make it last, the hours of glorious acceptance. Often an agent/editor phones you to offer a personal acceptance. It's an equally special moment for an agent/editor. After so much searching, he or she has finally discovered another worthy book. For most, it's a joy to announce, "I like it. I want it. I believe in you."

Your new agent or editor may have phoned for other reasons as well. Stay on your toes and be prepared for discussion of strategies or terms. Take good notes, but don't commit to anything important; instead, insist on time to mull over everything.

QUESTIONS FOR YOUR AGENT/EDITOR

If an agent has accepted your proposal and wants to represent you, now is the time to articulate concerns about his or her range of experience, business methods, and communication style. For instance, here are some questions to ask an agent, on the phone or in writing, prior to agreeing to representation:

1. Which publishers are you thinking about contacting? How many proposals do you send to start with? How many publishers do you try, on the average, before you give up?
2. How often can I expect to hear from you? Will you send me copies of rejection letters as you get them? Will you apprise me of your marketing strategies and, in general, keep in frequent contact? Or not?
3. What fees, if any, can I expect to pay? How is this handled? How do you manage the receipt of advances and royalties? Do you set up separate accounts for each author? Do you pay immediately upon receipt of monies from the publisher?
4. May I have a list of your recent sales in nonfiction? May I contact several of your current clients? Do you have any brochures about your agency?
5. Do you have a written contract that spells out each of our rights and responsibilities and explains how either of us can terminate this relationship? Would you send a sample contract?

If you have been offered a contract by an editor directly, you may want to ask these questions and others.

1. What advance are you offering? What royalty rate? When will the advance be paid out?
2. How big a print run do you plan?

3. How much will my book sell for? Will it come out in hardback, trade paperback, or mass market?
4. Will you recommend three to five agents whom you hold in high regard?

If you intend to use an agent, refrain from any discussion of an advance, even if an editor brings it up and pushes you for a decision.

Contract details are the domain of your agent who can't negotiate on anything you've committed to. An agent can nearly always secure a better contract, including a higher advance or better royalty. An agent can also protect you from unscrupulous publishers who take advantage of the moment to gain your verbal agreement.

> In publishing, verbal agreements are legally binding.

To protect yourself, prepare a script for the day you get your acceptance call. Say something like, "I'm truly excited by your offer. You've given me a lot to think about. I'll get back to you within forty-eight hours." The consequences are too serious for you not to postpone your decision. Your best defense against ignorance or gullibility is to become informed. Once you have an agent, he or she can answer your questions. Even so, learn as much as you can. Three ways are to read books on the subject, talk with published authors, and meet editors and agents at conferences. Check the Resource Directory at the end of this book for other helpful books on the industry.

> Agree to nothing until you think over the offer and, possibly, consult with an agent.

Special Considerations

The greatest problem faced by writers in deciding whether to seek agent representation comes with assessing accurately the size of the market. To a great extent, the type of book you are writing will aim you toward either an agent or an editor. Books written for a narrow audience, books of a specialized nature, such as this one, or an instructional guide for teachers, or a religious book, or a nonfiction book for children typically require no agent help.

AN AGENT'S EXPENSES

Some agent expenses averaged over all clients produce a cost per author of $600–800. If you step into an agent's shoes, you'd evaluate each book based upon whether you can recoup that $800 in expenses and make a profit. Since narrow-interest books usually involve modest print runs of 3000 to 5000 copies at most, the arithmetic produces a grim picture from an agent's viewpoint. Let's say your author royalty is $1 per copy. On this print run, you'd make $3000–5000 if all books sell. The standard agent commission is 15 percent of your gross. That's $400–750 when the last book is sold.

Because of financial reality, most agents sell only to the mid- to large-sized publishers, and they take on only books that support a strong market. The staple sales for any agency are solid and large markets, such as books on business, parenting, how-to, self-help, celebrity biography, and other wide markets.

ASSESSING YOUR BOOK'S PLACE

One of the most difficult decisions for many writers is determining whether a book idea is too specialized to seek an agent and expect publication with a major house. It's not an easy judgment call. Your best insurance in judging correctly is to follow the advice in chapter two about evaluating your idea; talk with booksellers and compare your book against the competition, and do an in-depth assessment of your market.

TESTING THE MARKET

Initially, I believed that Jan G. Jett had a large market for her book on profitable tour escorting. I considered the cresting tsunami of baby boomers as evidence of an up-and-coming large market. After all, as they retire they'll use their leisure time to travel more. Jan agreed and queried large and mid-sized publishers. Only one, a vocational book publisher, considered her proposal seriously enough to hash it over in an editorial committee. In the end, she earned praise for the proposal and for the book concept, but a rejection because of the perceived narrow market. Jan's solution? She became an independent publisher selling her tour-escort book through direct mail.

When Dr. McGuire, author of the proposed book, *Moved to Tears*, secured agent representation for her book, the agent believed they would find a large market and editors eager to publish it. Although editor comment was positive about Dr. McGuire's ability to write, it was lukewarm about the book's concept. "Women believe they know how to cry, and men aren't interested," said many editors. Dr. McGuire and her agent concluded that she might be ahead of the culture; however, to publish now, she would have to broaden her book's scope beyond tears.

For every rule in publishing, exceptions abound. Perceived large-market books might not sell well and perceived small-market books might become bestsellers. The five authors of the book on twins feared their book would be seen as serving a small, specialized market. They decided to test the possibilities by sending a query to ten large publishing houses. One requested the proposal but ultimately rejected the book as "not quite right for us." However, the editor was enthusiastic enough to recommend agent Carol Abel whom she knew had particular interest in the twin topic. Ms. Abel became their agent and made the sale within three months to Fireside, an imprint of Simon & Schuster, just as the company was planning the development of a birthing-related line of books. They needed *one* book on twins. Now in its second printing, the book sold out its first 10,000 copies. It's still a special-interest book to a highly targeted audience, but it has found a large enough market to sustain it. Their book is evidence of the maxim, "In publishing, timing is everything."

Reclaiming Perspective

Once you sign a contract, you can shift your perspective from the book's potential, what it might do once it comes out, to the necessity of writing it to the best of your ability. In the contract-negotiation phase of a book deal, it's easy to be swept into the bigger world of profits and praise. Now is the time to narrow your focus on the reason you did all this: to write your book.

You have much to look forward to, including the satisfying moment when a reader lets you know how he or she has been helped, persuaded, or entertained by your book. I enjoyed that moment with the book that launched my own publishing career, one that I had self-published. In 1980 I wrote about Mabel Dzata, a midwife from Ghana, Africa, who had delivered my two children by home birth. The book began as a thank-you and memory book and ended with birth stories of a dozen families spanning 158 pages and a first print run of 2600 copies.

Ten years after its publication, I attended a reunion picnic for Mabel at a park, attended by dozens of her families. The children ran and played, unaware of their parents' gratitude to the woman with healing hands who had "caught" them. I saw one mother twenty years younger than myself clutching a much-used copy of my book. I didn't tell her who I was, but couldn't resist asking her about the book. She said, "It got me through the birth of my girl. I want Mabel to sign it." Her words were payment beyond any royalty, satisfaction to fill my soul.

I couldn't wish you more.

Appendices

Proposal Writers Who Contributed to This Book and the Status of Their Books

Body Salts: A Way to Health Naturally
(holistic medicine, reference)
Dr. Skye Weintraub, N.D.
Complementary Medicine Publishing Co., Portland, OR. 1993, $20.
No agent.

> Sold through retail outlets that sell natural foods and supplements, and through direct mail to other holistic practitioners. Dr. Weintraub is expecting a 1995 release of her second book, with a working title of *Minding Your Body: A Comprehensive Guide to Natural Living in an Unnatural Environment.*

Cheapskate Decorating
(craft, how-to)
Aline Renauld Prince, decorator and instructor

> Finished as a proposal just before this book went to press, the author recieved an enthusiastic request for the proposal from an agent and awaits a decision on her proposal.

Creating Eden: The Garden As A Healing Space
(self-help, nature, ecology)
Psychotherapist Marilyn Barrett, Ph.D.
HarperCollins, 1992, $18.
Literary agent: Natasha Kern
Dr. Barrett is working on a second book, while continuing to actively promote her first.

Five Days to an Organized Life

(business)

Lucy H. Hedrick, time management and business consultant

Bantam Doubleday Dell Publishing Group Inc., 1990, $8.95 U.S., $11.95 Canada; over 80,000 sold.

Literary agent: Denise Marcil

Susbsequent books: *365 Ways to Save Time* ('92); *365 Ways to Save Time With Kids* ('93); *365 Ways to Save Money* ('94): all three sell for $10 and are published by The Hearst Group, a division of William Morrow Publishing Co.

The Fourth Era: Energy From Space

(science, energy technologies)

Ralph Nansen, former Boeing Solar Power Satellite Program Manager

Ocean Press, 910 Tall Ships Court SW, Ocean Shores, WA 98569 (206)289-3201

> The proposal was at first represented by an agent and marketed to large publishers. When it did not land a large publisher, the author decided to independently publish rather than market to small or specialized publishers. By some of the reasons for rejection, he determined that his ideas may have been too much at the cutting edge for editorial risk. With all of his contacts in and out of the aerospace industry, Ralph Nansen believes he'll reach his market and sell enough copies to interest a large publisher in a subsequent edition. You may reach the author at the above address for his book or to inquire about securing this rocket scientist for a speaking engagement.

Grammar for Grownups

(grammar, how-to, reference)

Val Dumond, business writing consultant and freelance editor

HarperCollins, 1994. $8, pb, $20 hb.

Literary agent: Denise Marcil

Previous book: *Elements of Non-Sexist Usage* (Prentice-Hall, 1991, $4.95)

The Hidden Life of Language

(language education)

Rosemarie Ostler, Ph.D., linguistics educator

Proposal represented by literary agent Carol Mann.

   Author is working on a book on linguistic origins' controversies.

Lifting the Veil: The Feminine Face of Science

(new science)

Linda Jean Shepherd, Ph.D., biochemist

Shambhala Publications, 1993, $14.00 pb.

Literary agent: Natasha Kern

   First edition of 6500 copies nearly sold out. Book captured 1994
   Washington State Governor's Literary Award. Author is at work
   on a novel!

Mothering Twins: From Hearing the News to Beyond the Terrible Twos

(birth, parenting, family)

Linda Albi, Deborah Johnson, Debra Catlin, Donna Florien Deurloo,
Sheryll Greatwood

Fireside, Simon & Schuster, 1993, $13.00pb.

Literary agent: Carol Abel

   Having sold out the first 10,000 copies, the book is in its second
   printing and going strong.

Moved to Tears: The Meaning and Joy in Learning to Cry

(how-to psychology)

Dr. Kathleen N. McGuire, Ph.D., psychologist

   At first, her proposal was enthusiastically represented by an agent
   and circulated to large publishers. Because of feedback about the
   book having a shaky market because of its focus on crying, this
   version of the proposal was turned back to the author. She is
   currently revamping it for a broader focus on "Focusing," a therapeutic technique at the heart of her practice.

Mysteries of the Dark Moon: The Healing Power of the Dark Goddess
(self-help, women's psychology, astrology)
Demetra George, counselor, mythologist and astrologer
HarperCollins, 1992, $15.
Literary Agent: Natasha Kern

> Strong sales as the author's third book, and accompanied by a workbook book published and sold separately by A.C.S. Publishers. Demetra George anticipates the publication of her fourth book in fall 1995 called: *Finding Our Way Through the Dark*. It is an astrological companion to *Mysteries of the Dark Moon*. Previous books: *Asteroid Goddess* (A.C.S. 1986) and *Astrology for Yourself* (Wingbow Press 1987).

No Pictures in My Grave: A Spiritual Journey in Sicily
(autobiography/inner journey, travel)
Susan Lloyd
Mercury House, 1992, $12.95pb. U.S.; $16.95 Canada.
Literary agent: Natasha Kern

> In addition to this literary nonfiction book, the author produced a documentary on her experience, "Processione: A Sicilian Easter," which won the 1990 American Film Festival award, the American Anthropological Association Society for Visual Anthropology award, the Vitas Film Festival of Folklore and Popular Culture 1991 'Best' award, and the Bronze Apple with the National Educational Film and Video Festival.

Organic Parenting: Raising Real People Through the Art of Human Relating, Birth to Six (Parenting)
Dean Walker, counselor and child development specialist.
Proposal represented by agent Bobbie Segal.

The Practical Woman's Guide to Real Estate Investment
(real estate)
Mabel Armstrong, real-estate investor and instructor

> Proposal was finished just as this book went to press. Author has begun the query process in search of an agent or editor.

Profitable Tour Escorting: A Comprehensive Guide

(travel, how-to)

Jan G. Jett, tour-escort instructor

Fox Hollow Press, 5477 Donald #13, Eugene, OR 97405, 1992, $14.95 pp, unbound edition

> Told by an agent that her book's scope was too narrow for agent representation or sale to large publishers, Jan still tried marketing her proposal on her own (and at my encouragement). Although it made it to editorial review committee with one publisher of career books, the agent's assessment proved correct. Still believing in her book, Jan founded her own press and has been successfully selling her book through direct mail.

Stop Being Manipulated: How to Neutralize the Bullies, Bosses, and Brutes in Your Life

(self-help psychology)

Dr. George H. Green and Carolyn Cotter, M.B.A.

Berkley Publishing Group, 1995, $4.95 U.S., $6.50 Canada, mass pb

Literary agent: Denise Marcil

> From proposal to finding an agent to contract spanned a five-year-period, testimony to the importance of persistence. While promoting their first book, co-author Carolyn Cotter is open to working with other qualified experts.

Stop Your Husband From Snoring: A Medically Proven Program to Cure the Night's Worst Nuisance

(medicine, how-to)

Dr. Derek S. Lipman, M.D.

Rodale Press, 1990, $7.95, out-of-print

Literary agent: David Morgan

> Although a success by any measure with over 30,000 books sold, and sales in four foreign countries, including two translations, Dr. Lipman was nevertheless disappointed by his publisher's choice of titles, which he felt was "narrow, politically-incorrect and downright offensive." The book is presently out-of-print and the rights have been released back to the author. With the resurgence of public interest in sleeping disorders and new research, Dr. Lipman secured an agent, received substantial offers from two big New

York houses who then withdrew the offers when it was discovered that a remaindering company had purchased those rights from Rodale and was still selling the book. In essence, Dr. Lipman's new book would be competing against his old one. Presently, he is updating the book and has interest by a small press specializing in health-related books. His new working title is: *Snoring From A to Zzzz: A Physician's Guide to Curing the Night's Worst Nuisance.*

Sudden Impact: Spontaneous Events That Shape Children's Lives
(education, psychology)
Dr. Michael Rousell, Ph.D., teacher, psychologist, hypnotist
  Proposal represented by literary agent Julia Castiglia.

Tales From Coon Creek Farm
(autobiography/literary)
Barbara Stevens-Newcomb, storyteller and artist
  Author just finished proposal and has begun marketing to agents and publishers. Through the author's personal memories, this literary nonfiction book seeks to awaken the reader's own sense of place, allowing the reader to recapture the fundamental questions of youth.

We'll Remember in November: Molly Yard's Gift to Women's Rights
(biography, women's history)
Emily Kay and Anita Saville, activists and members of N.O.W.
Literary agent: Natasha Kern
Sold to Prometheus Books.

The Last Zapatista
(latino history, travel, personal experience)
Literary agent: Natasha Kern
  Susan Lloyd, author, photographer, film-maker, lay historian. Proposal under revision to widen scope to the zapatista uprising, not just to its namesake. The author has recently finished a documentary film on Zapata.

Resource Directory

On the World of Publishing

Balkin, Richard. *A Writer's Guide to Book Publishing*, third edition revised by Nick Bakalar and Richard Balkin. New York, NY: Plume/Penguin Group, 1994. As the author says, "This book presumes to contain most of what…a potential author might want to know about publishing." Clear and well-written, this book does exactly that.

Balkin, Richard. *A Writer's Guide to Contract Negotiations*. Cincinnati: Writer's Digest Books, 1985. This short book has no fluff, yet provides a thorough explanation of every clause in a standard book contract. Written by a literary agent, this guide presents negotiating strategies that will help you understand what your agent is doing or help you negotiate your own contract.

Beren, Peter and Brad Bunnin, *Writer's Legal Companion*, second edition revised. Reading, MA: Addison-Weseley Publishing Co., 1993. Two lawyers offer explanations of publishing law, including contracts, copyrights, permissions, libel, subsidiary rights, agent agreements and more.

Collier, Oscar and Frances Spatz Leighton. *How to Write and Sell Your First Nonfiction Book*, first paperback edition. NY: St. Martin's Press, 1994. While the proposal process is swept over in a single chapter, the rest of the book offers good advice on the world of agents, editors, and selling. The authors also offer a practical advice for how to write your book once you have a contract.

Directory of Portable Databases, semi-annual. Detroit, MI: Gale Research Inc. Provides access to what's available on CD-ROM, diskettes, and magnetic tapes. Summarizes 2000 databases.

Gross, Gerald, editor. *Editors on Editing: What Writers Need to Know About What Editors Do*, third edition. NY: Grove Press, 1993. Comments by many of the most prestigious editors in the business. Addresses all aspects of editing—structural, theoretical, practical—with wit and insight. This anthology is incomparable in building an historical understanding of this complex and arcane industry.

Kirsch, Jonathan, *Kirsch's Handbook of Publishing Law*. Venice, CA: Acrobat, 1995. Written by a lawyer who is also a novelist, this handbook clarifies your rights and responsibilities as a writer. It explains contracts, documentation of research and sources, legal protections of confidential sources, copyright and "fair use" laws, defamation, and invasion of privacy. Also covers electronic and subsidiary rights, and often overlooked rights that occur with the end of your book's life.

Mandell, Judy. *Book Editors Talk to Writers*. New York, NY: John Wiley & Sons, Inc., 1995. Covering every aspect of publishing that would interest nonfiction or fiction writers, this book's question-and-answer format grants accessibility of the information and feels like the editors are talking directly to the reader. This book features penetrating interviews with 44 experienced editors, and includes discussions about the cutting-edge technologies, called "new media." I couldn't put it down!

Poynter, Dan. *The Self-Publishing Manual: How to Write, Publish and Sell Your Own Book*, eighth edition. Santa Barbara, CA: Para Publishing, 1995. Although written for the self-publisher, this classic offers easy-to-understand and up-to-date information on promotion, publicity, distribution and use of fax, CD-ROMs, and information-system bookstores for book sales.

Ross, Marilyn, and Tom Ross. *The Complete Guide to Self-Publishing*, third edition. Cincinnati, OH: Writer's Digest Books, 1994. Even though you may not wish to self-publish, this comprehensive guide offers good information on selecting a marketable topic, "product development," organizing and editing your manuscript, and on promotion.

Stengl, Jean. *How to Get Your Teaching Ideas Published: A Writer's Guide to Educational Publishing*, New York, NY: Walker & Co., 1994. A specialty guidebook offering the steps and resources to connect teacher/writer with educational publisher.

Reference Books to Find Other Books on Your Subject

Book Review Digest. Monthly (except February and July), Bronx, NY: H.W. Wilson. Summaries of original book reviews from about 100 popular and scholarly periodicals. If you find a competitor's book featured, you save yourself the time of running down book reviews in separate sources.

Book Review Index. Detroit, MI: Gale Research Inc. Master Indexed by author and title. Cumulations from 1965-1984 and from 1985-current. Nearly 2 million review citations from about 200 periodicals. Great way to look up books that might be competitors for "About the Competition."

Books in Print. Annual. New Providence, RI: R.R. Bowker. Indexed by author, title, and subject, these volumes index over 1 million books in the U.S. from 40,000 publishers and distributors.

Books Out-of-Print. Annual. New Providence, RI: R.R. Bowker. Important to check by subject and cross-reference by synonyms so that you can find other books published on your subject within the last five years—for "About the Competition," and to keep abreast in your field.

British Books in Print: The Reference Catalogue of Current Literature. Annual. London: J. Whitaker & Sons. (distributed in the U.S. by R.R. Bowker).

Business and Economics Books and Serials in Print, published irregularly. New Providence, RI: R.R. Bowker.

Canadian Books in Print. Annual. Toronto ON: University of Toronto Press. Indexed by author and title and with a subject index.

Children's Books in Print. Annual. New Providence, RI: R.R. Bowker. An author, illustrator, and title index to some 88,000 books available in the U.S. and written for children.

Computer Books and Serials in Print, published annually. New Providence, RI: R.R. Bowker.

Forthcoming Books, published bi-monthly, New Providence, RI: R.R.

Bowker. Use this index to nab books for your "About the Competition" that will be published in the next six months.

Medical and Health Care Books and Serials in Print. Annual. New Providence, RI: R.R. Bowker. Index of 62,000 books in the U.S. by title and author in 5000 subject areas. Also, 11,000 serials worldwide by title and subject.

Paperbound Books in Print. Semi-annual (spring and fall). New Providence, RI: R.R. Bowker. Author, title, and subject indexes to all in-print and forthcoming paperback books: trade and text, adult and juvenile, scholarly and mass market. Although Books in Print includes some paperbound books, this index will supply missing books in print on your subject.

Religious Books and Serials in Print: An Index to Religious Literature Including Philosophy. Biennial (in fall). New Providence, RI: R.R. Bowker.

Scientific and Technical Books and Serials in Print. Annual. New Providence, RI: R.R. Bowker. Author, title, and subject indexes to over 148,000 books in 14,500 subject areas on science and technology available in the U.S. Title and subject guides included for 26,000 serials in some 600 subject areas.

Small Press Record of Books in Print. Annual. Paradise, CA: Dustbooks. Editor, Len Fulton. Offers full in-print listings of 30,000 books in more than 2500 of the world's small presses.

Subject Guide to Books in Print. Annual. New Providence, RI: R.R. Bowker. As a companion volume to *Books in Print*, this volume indexes 830,000 in-print nonfiction books of over 41,000 U.S. publishers and distributors, using 72,000 Library of Congress headings and 60,000 cross-references. You may also find a *Subject Guide to Children's Books in Print*, and a *Subject Guide to Forthcoming Books in Print*.

On Research

Berkman, Robert I. *Find It Fast: How to Uncover Expert Information on Any Subject*, third edition, updated and revised. New York: HarperCollins, 1994. This book streamlines the research process. You'll learn not only how to locate experts, interview, take notes, and evaluate information, but you'll also find solid introductory information on auto-mated CD-ROM systems, consumer on-line services and Internet.

Directory of Directories. Series. Detroit, MI: Gale Research Inc., 1987. Identifies directories in subject categories and lists bibliographies. Described by researcher Lois Horowitz as "one-stop-shopping in the research world."

The Gale Directory of Publications and Broadcast Media. Annual. Detroit, MI: Gale Research Inc. Arranged by state, province, and city with demographics given for each city, this directory provides informa-tion on periodicals and broadcast media, but not books.

Horowitz, Lois. *Knowing Where to Look: The Ultimate Guide to Research.* Cincinnati, OH: Writer's Digest Books, 1984. This is my favorite book on research. Written well. Organized well. It's actually *interest-ing* to read and lives up to its promise as "the ultimate guide."

The Reader's Guide to Periodical Literature. I've included this only to sug-gest that you exclude it from your research. This guide is probably the one you are most familiar with from school research. However, it only indexes about 180 magazines. Nowadays, there are so many indexes that are better, larger, and more-subject specific.

Standard Periodical Directory. Annual. New York, NY: Oxbridge Com-munications Inc. Lists 90,000 U.S. and Canadian periodicals arranged by subject matter into 230 classifications and indexed by title. This directory makes it difficult to claim your subject has "never been done!"

Statistical Sources. Issued every 5–7 years. Edited by Paul Wasserman and Jacqueline O'Brien. Detroit, MI: Gale Research Inc. This refer-ence book offers a bibliography of about 150 statistics publications in industry, government, business, social sciences, and finances. This will help you narrow your references by subject, sending you to particular sources for the actual statistics.

Statistical Abstract of the United States. Annual. Washington, D.C: U.S. Dept. of Government, Bureau of the Census. This provides the sta-tistical answers to Census questions of a political, social, and eco-nomic nature.

American Statistics Index. Washington D.C: Congressional Information Service. This is a comprehensive index to 3000 statistical directories published by federal and state agencies, commercial publishers, and intergovernmental organizations.

Ulrich's International Periodical Directory. Annual. New Providence, NJ: R.R. Bowker. A subject-arranged list of more than 140,000 active periodicals, irregular serials, and annuals published throughout the world. A great help to comprehensive research of what's reaching the general public and the specialist reader.

On Writing and Editing

Adams, Deborah M. and Jeff Herman. *Write the Perfect Book Proposal: 10 Proposals That Sold and Why*. New York: John Wiley & Sons Inc., 1993. An excellent companion book on proposals that features ten complete proposals with marginal comments.

Bates, Jefferson D. *Writing With Precision: How to Write So That You Cannot Possibly Be Misunderstood*. Herndon, VA: Acropolis Books Ltd., 1990. This is a super book to guide you through self-editing. Checklists, clear headings, and exercises allow you to pull out what you need. Sections have been added for the computer age and include organizing, file management, and word processing.

Bennett, Hal Z. *How to Write With a Collaborator*. Cincinnati, OH: Writer's Digest Books, 1988. Helpful guidelines to anyone who plans to team up with another writer, an expert, or a celebrity to co-author books, articles, and short stories.

Cheney, Theodore A. Rees. *Getting the Words Right: How to Revise, Edit & Rewrite*. Cincinnati, OH: Writer's Digest Books, 1983. If you want to delve into editing, this book will take you on an extensive journey into craft. Less of a shopping mall of easy-fix editing ideas, this book will give you the fundamental concepts to make you an all-round better writer.

The Chicago Manual of Style, thirteen edition. Chicago, IL: University of Chicago Press, 1982. Long considered the 'last word' in editorial disputes, I couldn't live, i.e. edit, without it. While you can use other more reader-friendly guidebooks—like *Pinckert's Practical Grammar* (listed below), *The Chicago Manual of Style* gives you the security of answering every conceivable question and trusting the source.

Cool, Lisa Collier. *How to Write Irresistible Query Letters*. Cincinnati, OH: Writer's Digest Books, 1987. Although primarily focused upon writing queries for magazine articles, this book lets you know how all queries are structured and what they are meant to accomplish.

Dumond, Val. *Grammar for Grownups: A Guide to Grammar and Usage for Everyone Who Has to Put Words on Paper Effectively*. New York: Harper-Collins, 1993. What I love about Val's book is the feeling of sitting down with her across my kitchen table and learning about grammar. She brings her own voice and personality into this normally dry subject matter, using colorful examples from adult experience.

Franklin, Jon. *Writing for Story: Craft Secrets of Dramatic Nonfiction by a Two-Time Pulitzer Prize Winner*. New York, NY: NAL, 1986. The subtitle says it all. A must read if you intend to write narrative, personal-experience, travel, or true-crime books. Franklin's method shows you how to borrow the dramatic structure of fiction and apply it to nonfiction.

Goldberg, Natalie. *Writing Down the Bones: Freeing the Writer Within*. Boston MS: Shambhala Publications, 1986. For inspiration and perspective, pick this book up and open it to any page. It will help rekindle the passion at moments when the many proposal requirements make you forget why you wanted to write a book.

Henson, Kenneth T. *The Art of Writing for Publication*. Needham Heights, MA: Simon & Schuster, 1995. Terrific book for everyone, but especially for writers steeped in academic or technical jargon. This book will lead you from dissertation writing to writing for journals to book publication with university presses and then to professional writing of trade books for the public. Also includes grant proposal writing.

Judd, Karen. *Copyediting, A Practical Guide*, second edition. Menlo Park, CA: Crisp Publications Inc., 1990. For authors, publishing personnel, writers, editors, journalists, teachers, desktop publishers, and computer software workers. Learn to recognize and use all those squiggly marks and produce clean, clear, copy.

Klauser, Henriette Anne. *Writing on Both Sides of the Brain: Breakthrough Techniques for People Who Write*. San Francisco, CA: Harper San Francisco, 1987. Inspiration and also practical techniques to bulldoze "writer's block" and to silence The Critic during production of your proposal.

Lane, Lea. *Steps to Better Writing: A Guide to the Process*. New York, NY: St. Martin's Press, 1983. If I had the power, I'd make this one of two required 'how to write' companions to my proposal book. (For the other one, see listing under Gary Provost.) Written textbook style, you'll learn details about researching your project, outlining it, understanding the methods of organization, and writing and refining it. This book provides a comprehensive brush-up on basic writing.

Markel, Michael H. *Technical Writing Situations and Strategies*. second edition. NY: St. Martin's Press, 1988. Use this to organize your research, select a method of organization, and outline your book.

The National Writers Club correspondence course in Freelance Writing. Suite 620, 1450 S. Havana, Aurora, CO 80012. I was an enrollee long ago. Their correspondence course is a great way to review the techniques of freelance writing, or learn how to write in the special style required for publication. You will also enjoy the benefit of a published teacher responding personally to your letters and lessons.

Pinckert, Robert C. *Pinckert's Practical Grammar: A Lively, Unintimidating Guide to Usage, Punctuation, and Style*. Cincinnati, OH: Writer's Digest Books, 1986. At last, review of "proper English" need be anything but proper. Pinckert makes it fun. Irreverent, funny examples put punctuation in its place. One of my favorite guides to usage, punctuation, and style.

Poynter, Dan, and Mindy Bingham. *Is There a Book Inside You? How to Successfully Author a Book Alone or Through a Collaborator*, fourth edition. Santa Barbara, CA: Para Publishing, 1991. A step-by-step formula for researching and writing a book, and how to find and work with a collaborator.

Provost, Gary, *Make Your Words Work*, Cincinnati, OH: Writers Digest Books, 1990. While I would have you study Lea Lane's *Steps to Better Writing* to clear out the cobwebs about basic writing, I would require Gary Provost's books for learning how to write popular non-fiction. His writing is proof of what he teaches; you're absorbed and entertained while learning.

Provost, Gary. *100 Ways to Improve Your Writing*. New York, NY: NAL, 1985. You'll take away *one thousand* ways to improve your writing. A must for any writer who is having trouble translating expert or technical vocabulary into everyday communication.

Roberts, Ellen. *Nonfiction for Children: How to Write It, How to Sell It*. Cincinnati, OH: Writer's Digest Books, 1986. With so few how-to books on writing nonfiction for children, this book stands out as the definitive work on the subject. It's also thorough, well-written, and offers as much to the writer of adult nonfiction as to the writer of children's nonfiction.

Writer's Digest correspondence course in nonfiction writing. 1507 Dana Ave., Cincinnati, OH 45207. Although I haven't sampled their nonfiction correspondence courses, I've heard positive testimonials from others who have. Correspondence courses offer a way to learn the techniques of writing for publication and have the benefit of a one-on-one relationship with an assigned teacher.

Zinsser, William. *On Writing Well*, fifth edition. New York, NY: HarperCollins, 1994. When I first started my writing career, I read Zinsser's book and practically enshrined it. It's simple, elegant, and inspiring. It's one of those books you can read again and again. His book set a standard to which I still aspire.

Market Guides to Find Publishers and Literary Agents

Anderson, Margaret J. *The Christian Writer's Handbook*. San Francisco: Harper San Francisco.

California and Hawaii Publishing Marketplace. Cupertino, CA: Writers Connection, 1990. A comprehensive directory of book publishers, magazines, literary agents, newspapers, organizations and conferences.

Children's Writer's & Illustrator's Market. Annual. Cincinnati, OH: Writer's Digest Books. Lisa Carpenter, editor. Comprehensive listing of children's book publishers and their specifications, including an age-level index. Also includes book and magazine markets for children writers and artists.

Herman, Jeff. *Insider's Guide to Book Editors, Publishers, and Literary Agents.* Annual. Rocklin, CA: Prima Publishing/St. Martin's Press, 1995. Not just a directory, this book provides a brief history of 400 United States and Canadian publishers that include large, university, and religious/spiritual publishers. The guide is unique in listing current names of some 1000 editors at these houses, by specialty. Part II features questionnaire answers by some 80 agents, answers that tell agent education and personal preferences, in addition to statistics about rejection rates, numbers of new authors represented in the past year, and numbers of titles sold in the past year.

Guide to Literary Agents. Annual. Cincinnati, OH: Writer's Digest Books. Providing the listings, contact names, and specifications of some 400 agents, this directory also provides the helpful division of fee-charging and non-fee charging agents, script agents, articles by agents, and indexes by subject and geographic location.

International Directory of Little Magazines and Small Presses. Annual, updated biannually. Len Fulton, editor. Paradise, CA: Dustbooks. Gives contact information and specifications on about 3500 markets, many of which are "tiny ventures" not listed elsewhere.

International Literary Market Place, updated annually. New Providence, RI: R.R. Bowker.

Lester, Meera. *Writing for the Ethnic Markets.* Cupertino, CA: Writers Connection, 1991. Provides writing tips, marketing strategies, and listings of book and magazine publishers and film and TV companies that buy ethnic material.

Literary Agents of North America. Annual. Author Aid/Research Associates International. Listing of approximately 1000 U.S. and Canadian literary agents, including their fees and commission rates, types of books represented, profiles of agency heads, number of clients, and specifications for queries or proposals.

Literary Market Place. Annual. New York: R.R. Bowker. Long considered "the bible" of the publishing industry, this tome lists over 40,000 companies and individuals in U.S. and Canadian publishing. It is divided into headings for book publishers, editorial services, literary agents, advertising, marketing, and publicity (including book clubs), direct mail specialists, magazines that feature books, book manufacturing, book distributors, wholesalers, book producers, services and supplies, awards, contests, and grants, book trade events, and much more.

New Choices for Writers: How to Get Published in the New Age Market. Elizabeth Gould, editor. Nantucket, MA: Writer's Resources, 1994. This selected directory includes about 50 publishers of new age and alternative books and gives specifications for each.

Publishers, Distributors, and Wholesalers of the United States. Annual. New Providence, RI: R.R. Bowker. A directory of some 64,500 active U.S. publishers, distributors, associations, and wholesalers, listing editorial and ordering addresses. Includes small and independent presses, producers of software, and audio cassettes by fields of activity.

Writers Northwest Handbook, sixth edition. Biennial. Portland: Media Weavers, 1995. Essays and how-to articles by writers comprise about one third of this handbook, while the rest offers the listings and specifications of some 3000 book and magazine publishers, as well as other resources for writers in the Pacific Northwest.

Writer's Market: Where to Sell, What to Write. Annual. Cincinnati, OH: Writer's Digest Books. Lists more than 4000 places where freelance writers can sell articles, books, novels, stories, fillers, scripts, and more. While you can get specifications and editor names for about 800 publishers, the 'Market' no longer includes agent listings.

On Promotion

Celebrity Directory, fifth edition. Biennial. Ann Arbor, MI: Axiom Information Resources, 1994. Described as a directory of over 7000 celebrities from entertainment to business who may be contacted for testimonials for the book trade. I wasn't able to find a copy of this, just a directory listing, so it may be similar to *Who's Who.*

Encyclopedia of Associations. Annual. Detroit, MI: Gale Research Inc. Arranged by topic, this guide lists more than 20,000 national organizations of the U.S. From this guide and the *National Trade and Professional Associations* guide, you can find groups where you can offer to promote your book. List these in "About the Market," and/or in "About Promotion." After you've written your book, follow up and offer yourself as a workshop or conference speaker. A librarian can help you check *Associations Reference File* on microform to actually see the full text of brochures and official literature offered by organizations listed in the *E.A.*

The Guide to Writer's Conferences, Shaw Associates, Suite 1406, Biltmore Way, Coral Gables, FL 33134.

Kremer, John. *1001 Ways to Market Your Books—For Authors and Publishers*. Fairfield, IA: Open Horizons Publishing Co., 1993. This book could have been titled 'Everything You Ever Needed to Know to Write a Great Promotions Section in Your Proposal.' Includes planning and design, advertising, distribution, subsidiary rights, and spin-offs.

National Trade and Professional Associations of the United States. Annual. Washington D.C.: Columbia Books, Inc. Gives data on 7500 trade associations, professional societies, and labor unions with national memberships. Uses broad subject headings in its index.

Parinello, Al. *On the Air: How to Get on Radio and TV Talk Shows and What to Do When You Get There*. Hawthorne, NJ: Career Press.

Rochester, Larry. *Book Publicity for Authors and Publishers*. Fall River Mills, CA: Sunset Hill, 1992.

Ross, Marilyn, and Tom Ross. *Marketing Your Books: A Collection of Profit-Making Ideas for Authors and Publishers*. Buena Vista, CO: Communication Creativity, 1990. Authors detail winning strategies for promoting and selling books and generating author publicity.

Publication Consent Agreement

I hereby give _____

author of _____

(working title of what is henceforth referred to as the Property), the absolute right and permission to copyright and/or publish or to have copyrighted or have published information about me contained in the above mentioned Property. I understand that a pseudonym is being used in place of my real name and that other physical attributes have been fictionalized in order to protect my right to privacy.

I also hereby waive any right to inspect and/or approve not only the final edited-for-publication versions of the book, but also any advertising copy that may be used in connection therewith.

I also agree that _____ or the publisher shall have all the irrevocable and unconditional dramatic and subsidiary rights to the Property, and can cause an actor to depict actions in incidents related to, based upon, or adapted from me as depicted by the "character" based upon me in the above mentioned Property. Further, such adaptations may include fictional scenes, incidents or episodes based upon but not specifically included in the Property in preparation or production of a picture, and I waive all rights to the exploitation of such a picture in all media throughout the world, and in connection with customary advertising and publicity related there to.

I represent that I will not assert or institute any claim or action against _____ or the publisher or other purchaser of rights based on the Property, on the grounds that their use of the above-described rights violates my right of privacy or any other right belonging to me. Nothing contained herein shall be construed as prejudicial to any rights to which I may otherwise be entitled as a member of the public.

None of the warranties or indemnities I make pursuant to this Release or elsewhere herein shall extend to (a) any changes or additions made in the Property, or (b) any elements of the Property which are undertaken to fictionalize for dramatic purposes. I agree to indemnify and hold harmless the author, publisher, or subsidiary rights' purchasers from and against any claims arising from such Changes.

Date _____ Signature _____

Phone _____ Address _____

Date _____

Witness Signature _____

Index

About the Author

Elizabeth Lyon is a freelance editor through Lyon's Literary Services, the company she started in 1988. She works with writers from the United States and Canada, helping them with their proposals, queries, novels, and synopses. She leads four critique groups of writers in Eugene, Oregon, where she also teaches community college classes in writing. She gives presentations on proposals and novelcraft to organizations and conferences.

Born in Toledo, Ohio, she attended Arizona State University and Whittier College. She holds a masters degree in counseling from California Family Studies Center, the branch campus of Azusa Pacific College in California. She lives with her two children, Kris and Elaine, her husband Charley—a horror and suspense novelist, and her step-daughter Sara.

Readers may correspond with or reach the author through Blue Heron Publishing, Inc., 24450 Northwest Hansen Road., Hillsboro, OR 97124.